Collins

A REALLY BRITISH GUIDE TO BUSINESS ENGLISH

Tom Rees

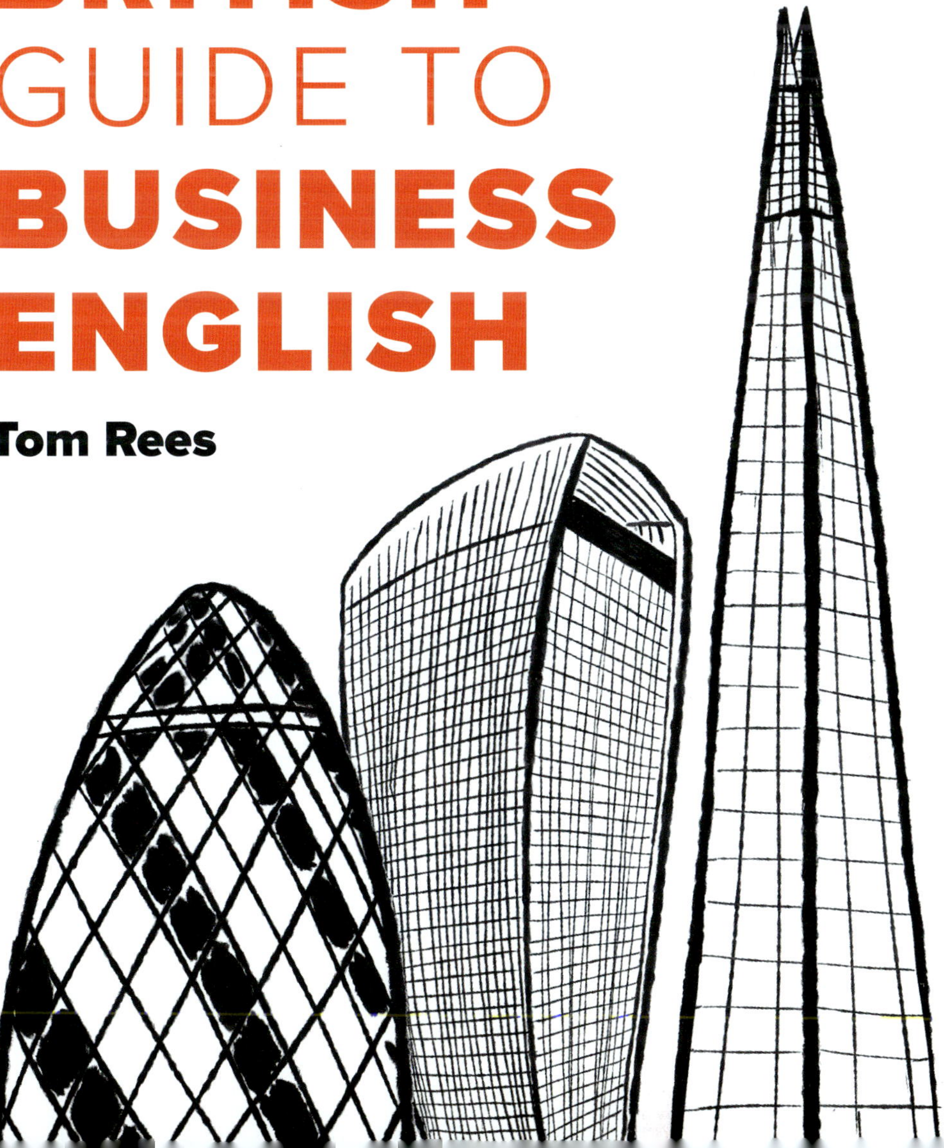

Published by Collins
An imprint of HarperCollins Publishers
1 Robroyston Gate
Glasgow
G33 1JN

HarperCollins Publishers
Macken House, 39/40 Mayor Street Upper,
Dublin 1, D01 C9W8 Ireland

First Edition 2026
Previously published as *A Really British Guide to Business English* by *EAT SLEEP DREAM ENGLISH*

10 9 8 7 6 5 4 3 2 1

ISBN 978-0-00-881135-8

Collins® is a registered trademark of HarperCollins Publishers Limited

collins.co.uk/elt

Typeset by Davidson Publishing Solutions, Glasgow

Printed in India

A catalogue record for this book is available from the British Library.

If you would like to comment on any aspect of this book, please contact us at the given address or online.
E-mail: collins.elt@harpercollins.co.uk

Acknowledgements

AUTHOR
Tom Rees

ILLUSTRATOR
Javier Joaquín (Beehive Illustration)

DESIGNERS
James Hunter
Kevin Robbins

FOR THE PUBLISHER
Kerry Ferguson
Fiona McGlade
Mary O'Neill

WITH SPECIAL THANKS TO
Ian Badger

MIX
Paper | Supporting responsible forestry
FSC™ C016779
www.fsc.org

Contents

LET'S GET STARTED

Introduction

I'd like you to picture the scene: You've just jumped on a call with your British colleagues when one of them cheerfully announces 'I need all hands on deck and everyone singing from the same hymn sheet, OK?', as if they've just said something perfectly normal. You nod, of course, while quietly wondering to yourself '*What on earth did any of that mean?*'

Welcome to British Business English – a world where indirectness, understatement and idiomatic phrasing all come together. It might feel a little confusing at first, but don't worry – I'll guide you through it, one phrase at a time.

The aim of this book is to provide you with the English that's actually used in offices and meeting rooms all over the UK. It's the English you'll find in emails, memos and presentations. It's the stuff you'll hear at business lunches, after-work socials and team bonding sessions. Essentially, it's your toolkit for understanding how people in modern British workplaces really speak.

As you work your way through the A–Z section, you'll come across hundreds of fabulous words, phrases, sayings and idioms. Many of them are everyday staples of Business English, while others might be industry-specific and a little more niche. I would encourage you to follow your curiosity for new vocabulary and self-select the ones that might be most useful in your working context. So many of them will be trusted friends you use over and over again, while others will remain strangers to you ... and that's OK.

During my long career teaching English around the world, I've come to realise that learning a language is all about connection: to the people, culture and environment around us. When we connect, we thrive; my sincerest hope is that this book will give you the tools to flourish in your working world, whatever that may be.

Happy reading,

Teacher Tom

ABOUT THE AUTHOR

Tom Rees is a London-based English educator and online content creator. He is the founder of Eat Sleep Dream English, a global platform helping students learn about the language and culture of the UK. His teaching career has taken him around the globe, from Spain and Argentina to Hong Kong and the UK.

ACKNOWLEDGEMENTS

This book could not have been possible without a few special people. First, I'd like to thank my Eat Sleep Dream English community of learners. I'm always humbled by how kind and supportive you all are. I'm constantly inspired to provide you with the best English language learning materials I can, and I hope this book helps you communicate more successfully in your working world.

I'd like to give a shout out to Fiona and Kerry at HarperCollins for putting their faith in me and helping this book come to life.

I owe a huge debt of gratitude to my dad and sister for their ongoing love and support. They have been my sounding boards and my biggest cheerleaders throughout this journey.

They say the apple doesn't fall far from the tree, and for me, it all starts with my mum. She was the one who inspired me to become a teacher and author. Witnessing her love of the English language set me off on this journey in 2007. Sadly, she passed away in 2017, but everything I have accomplished since then has had her gentle influence. This is for you, Mum.

Finally, I'd like to give a very special thanks to my wife, Shana, for her knowledge, support and inspiration. She has been an incredible resource for the contents of this book and guided me to create something of real benefit to my learners. On top of all that, she has been my anchor throughout this journey, helping me navigate the storms of business and life. I literally couldn't have done this without you.

How This Book Works

Here's a short guide to the different sections you'll find in the book:

WORK CULTURE IN THE UK

We start the book with a short guide to the business culture of the UK. What are the typical working hours? How many days of holiday do we get a year? What do we have for lunch? All of these questions, and more, are answered here.

A–Z OF BUSINESS ENGLISH WORDS AND PHRASES

We then move on to the main section of the book: the A–Z of Business English. I have collected hundreds of essential words and phrases that will help you navigate the working world. They range from wonderfully descriptive idioms to functional phrasal verbs, and everything in between. Each entry in the A–Z section has:

- a word or phrase
- the part of speech: noun, adjective, etc.
- the IPA phonetic script to help with pronunciation (not for idioms and phrases)
- the meaning
- an example sentence to put it into context.

Here's an example entry:

> **agile** (adjective) /ˈædʒaɪl/
> flexible, able to adapt quickly to feedback and rapidly learn.
> *'If our company is going to survive in this market, we need to become more agile.'*

This is by no means an exhaustive list of all the words and phrases you'll come across at work, but it is a collection of the essentials. A priority for me has been to include as many contemporary Business English words and phrases as possible. I want this book to reflect the English we really use in the modern workplaces of the UK. You'll find fun Britishisms like 'wiggle room' and 'move the goalposts'. alongside more international terms like 'A/B testing' and 'hot-desking'. My hope is that this section will act as a reference point for the language you'll see and hear around you.

You can listen to audio recordings of the words and phrases in the A–Z at **collins.co.uk/eltresources**

BUSINESS ACRONYMS

Our next section looks at the acronyms and initialisms we use in Business English. You'll find a long list of the shortened terms we use, from CEO to ROI.

MINI LESSONS

Finally, there are 17 Mini Lessons for you to work through at your leisure – eleven of these are in the book and the remaining six are online. Each one focuses on a functional aspect of communicating in Business English. For example, in Mini Lesson 2, we look at useful phrases to help you describe your role at work and the tasks and responsibilities you have. In Mini Lesson 11, we focus on some common phrases you might use to help you participate in meetings. The six online Mini Lessons (Mini Lessons 12–17) form an essential guide to writing professional emails. You can find these here:

The aim of these Mini Lessons is to provide some structure to your learning, and to test what you remember. There is also an answer section at the back of the book, so you can check what you have learned.

This book is designed to give you the English you need to win in the workplace, so when you are ready, let's begin!

WORK CULTURE IN THE UK

During my teaching career, I've worked in several countries around the world: the UK, Spain, Argentina and Hong Kong. In each one, I had to learn a new set of written and unwritten rules about how to conduct myself in the workplace. Customs that seemed so alien to me at the beginning became second nature by the end. The best example of this was in Argentina, where everyone greets each other, even strangers, with a kiss on the cheek. This came as a big shock to me in my first adult IELTS class when Guillermo, a 32-year-old accountant, walked in and greeted me with a kiss on the cheek. As the class entered the room, one by one, they all greeted me in the same way. Initially this felt quite odd, but by the end of the year I felt totally at ease with it, and in fact exported the custom home with me to the UK. Needless to say, it caused a little confusion for all the Brits I encountered.

So with this in mind, I wanted to document a few of the written and unwritten rules in the UK, so you know what to expect when working here.

HOURS

Generally speaking, people in the UK work eight hours a day, typically from 9 a.m. to 5 p.m. However, this can vary depending on the type of job and the company. In recent years, working hours have become much more flexible, giving people greater autonomy over when they complete their core hours. The legal limit that a company can ask its employees to work is 48 hours a week, averaged over a 17-week period. However, it is possible for a company to ask its employees to sign an opt-out agreement, therefore agreeing to work more hours. There are also exceptions to this limit for specific jobs like trainee doctors and oil-rig workers. The working week is Monday to Friday, but this will depend on the industry. If you work in hospitality, for example, you would probably be expected to work weekends.

NATIONAL MINIMUM WAGE AND LIVING WAGE

In the UK, workers are legally entitled to receive a minimum wage per hour, depending on how old they are. At the time of writing, the National Minimum Wage applies to anyone of school-leaving age and up to 20 years old. The National Living Wage applies to anyone 21 years old and above. You can find out what the current hourly rates are on the gov.uk website.

GREETINGS

As a general rule in the workplace, Brits shake hands to greet each other. This is true for colleagues meeting for the first time or for when you are meeting clients. On a day-to-day basis, there is no need to greet your colleagues with a handshake in the morning. A simple 'Hello' or 'How are you?' will suffice. Of course, this will depend on the workplace you are in and your relationships with your colleagues. A good rule of thumb is to take your cues from the people around you, and see what they do.

OFFICE CLOTHING

In this day and age, companies are a lot more relaxed about what their employees wear to work than in the past. Most people I spoke to said there weren't any specific rules about what they can and cannot wear. Having said that, they all understood the need to look professional at work, so most described their attire as 'smart casual'. A few spoke about how there was an expectation to dress more formally if they were doing any customer-facing or client-facing work that day. As always, the job, the company and the industry all play a part in dictating what one should wear to work.

HOLIDAY

Most workers in the UK are entitled to 28 days' paid annual leave if they work a five-day week. This equates to roughly 5.6 weeks a year. In England and Wales, there are usually eight bank holidays (i.e. public holidays) per year. The main ones are around Christmas and Easter, with a few dotted about in May and at the end of August. In Scotland, there is an extra day on 30th November to mark

St Andrew's Day, and in Northern Ireland there are two extra days: 17th March for St Patrick's Day and one in July to commemorate the Battle of the Boyne. Employers are not obliged to give their employees paid leave on public holidays. You can check when the next bank holiday is via the gov.uk website.

LUNCH

Lunchtime rituals are a sacred thing in many countries, but not in the UK. To my great surprise, almost all the people I surveyed said they eat lunch at their desks. Some said they sit with colleagues while eating, but the vast majority tended to work through their break. Lunch is taken between 11:30 a.m. and 2 p.m. and usually lasts for 30 minutes or an hour.

It's common practice in some industries to have a working lunch, during which business is discussed over a meal, often in a restaurant. An extension of a working lunch is a 'boozy lunch', in which alcohol is also consumed. This, however, has generally become a thing of the past for most industries.

'Did you know there's a magical little meal in between breakfast and lunch called "elevenses"? It's taken around, yes, you guessed it, 11 a.m., and it usually involves a cup of tea or coffee and something small to eat, like a snack bar or biscuit. As well as staving off hunger, it's also a great opportunity to get up from your desk, stretch your legs and maybe have a quick chat with a colleague. I'm a big fan!'

Teacher Tom

A standard office lunch consists of a sandwich, soup or salad. Many places offer 'meal deals' where you can get a sandwich, a snack and a drink for a set price. Of course, it's common for people to prepare their own lunch at home and bring it to work. Depending on where the office is, there is also a wide range of alternative options like pasta, burritos and sushi. One thing to be mindful of is bringing strong-smelling food to your desk. That said, most offices have communal kitchens or seating areas where you can go if need be.

SOCIALISING

One aspect that surprises people from abroad is how Brits conduct social business. For many cultures, socialising happens over a meal – in the UK, it's often in the pub.

After work, it's common for colleagues in the UK to head to the pub together to unwind, chat about their day and catch up on the latest football scores or trending TV shows. Walk through most city centres on a weekday evening – especially a Thursday – and you'll see pubs filled with after-work crowds. The saying 'Thursdays are the new Fridays' reflects how popular Thursday nights have become for socialising with colleagues.

More broadly, going to the pub is how Brits form social bonds. It's a way of life here that extends to work. That said, lots of people don't drink alcohol, for various reasons, and that doesn't stop them from participating in work socials. Indeed, these days, lots of companies are mindful to organise more inclusive events for all workers.

WORK–LIFE BALANCE

Finding that balance between working hard and enjoying your free time is something many of us struggle with. In my conversations with various people working in the UK, one thing quickly became evident: finding a good work–life balance is hugely important to everyone. Indeed, there is also a growing emphasis being placed on this by companies.

Presenteeism – the act of spending more time at work than you need to in order to prove your worth – is actively being discouraged in many workplaces. Ambition and drive are encouraged, but there is a sense that a healthy amount of downtime can actually help productivity, not hinder it. Mental health support in the workplace has improved dramatically in the last ten years, and the pandemic forced many companies to rethink how they supported their employees.

LANGUAGE

Communicating with colleagues is a huge part of almost every job, and in the UK it's critically important to be polite and professional. Brits are known for their indirectness, which is one tool we use to sound polite. There are a multitude of phrases you can employ to 'fluff up' your words and make them sound more polite. Mini Lesson 3 on page 100 is dedicated to this, but here are a few examples to give you an idea.

Direct: 'Open the window!'

Indirect: 'Would you mind opening the window?'

Direct: 'I don't know what to do. Help me!'

Indirect: 'I'm not sure what to do. I don't suppose you'd be able to help me, would you?'

Another important thing to remember is the use, or non-use, of swear words in a work environment. Of course there are exceptions, but as a general rule, the use of any swear word at work is frowned upon and should be avoided.

'There's definitely a big cultural difference between how Brits and Americans communicate. Brits tend to be less direct than their American counterparts, who are much more forthright and candid. It's something you'll need to be aware of when working in either context.'

Teacher Tom

ONE MORE THING

In my research, I asked people working here in the UK to give me one piece of advice for anyone coming to the UK to work. These are just a few of the things they mentioned:

FIND A WORKPLACE MENTOR

IF SOMETHING IS BOTHERING YOU, ADDRESS IT DIRECTLY AND CANDIDLY WITH YOUR LINE MANAGER

BE PUNCTUAL, POLITE AND SOCIALISE WHEN THERE'S A CHANCE

A FRIENDLY ATTITUDE GOES A LONG WAY

PUT (AND GET) EVERYTHING IN WRITING

A–Z OF BUSINESS ENGLISH WORDS AND PHRASES

A

A/B testing (noun) /eɪ ˈbiː ˌtestɪŋ/
a method of testing two versions of the same thing with an audience, to see which one performs better.
'We've used A/B testing to find out which thumbnail works best and it was the one with the blue text.'

accountable (adjective) /əˈkaʊntəbəl/
if someone is accountable for something, they are responsible and must be able to give reasons for their actions.
'Ultimately, we are accountable to the shareholders.'

across (something) (phrase) /əˈkrɒs/
understanding something fully.
'Eva is across the report, so maybe it's best to send her an email if you have any questions.'

across the board (idiom)
involving or affecting everyone.
'A 4% pay rise will be applied across the board.'

action (something) (verb) /ˈækʃən/
to deal with something or make it happen.
'Roberto, can you action these contracts for me?'

action item (noun) /ˈækʃən ˌaɪtəm/
a specific task or objective that needs to be done. It usually comes as a result of a meeting.
'Sorry I missed the meeting. Are there any big action items I can help with?'

add colour to (something) (idiom)
to add details or more context to a piece of work.
'Patrick, can you add some colour to this presentation? It's lacking some key details like subscriber growth and click-through rates.'

ad hoc (adverb/adjective) /ˌæd ˈhɒk/
if something is done ad hoc, it is only done when necessary or needed.
'We'll create the social media posts on an ad hoc basis.'

Audio for the words and phrases in the A-Z can be found at **collins.co.uk/eltresources**

admin (noun) /ˈædmɪn/
the organisational tasks that need to be done, e.g. completing forms or making travel arrangements (short for ‘administration’).
‘I’ve just got a bit of admin to do and then I’ll be ready to go.’

agile (adjective) /ˈædʒaɪl/
flexible, able to adapt quickly to feedback and rapidly learn.
‘If our company is going to survive in this market, we need to become more agile.’

ahead of the curve (idiom)
more advanced and ahead of current ways of doing something.
‘The technology Microsoft was using back then was ahead of the curve.’

a leg-up (idiom)
if you get/have a leg-up, you receive the help you need to get an advantage over others to achieve something (also ‘give (someone) a leg-up’).
‘He’s had a massive leg-up in life because his family are extraordinarily rich and his father owns the company.’

align (with something) (verb) /əˈlaɪn/
to support or agree with something.
‘Some of the things this company has done in the past don’t align with my values.’

all-expenses-paid (adjective) /ɔːlɪkspensɪsˈpeɪd/
if something is all-expenses-paid, it is completely paid for by a company.
‘The company is flying me out to an all-expenses-paid training course in Copenhagen.’

all (one’s) eggs in one basket (idiom)
if you put all your eggs in one basket, you put all your effort and resources into one idea or project.
‘As an investor, I don’t like to put all my eggs in one basket.’

all hands on deck (idiom)
everyone is required to work hard on something in order to get it done (also ‘all hands to the pump’).
‘We’ve got to get the Gucci ad campaign finished by Friday, so we need all hands on deck.’

‘The etymology of “all hands on deck” has an old naval connection. To navigate a ship through a storm, the captain would demand all the hands (sailors) go on deck and help steer it, hence the term we have today.’
Teacher Tom

along (those/these) lines (phrase)
similar to (also 'along the lines of …').
'My old flatmate just retrained as a pastry chef; I'd love to do something along those lines.'

anchor day (noun) /ˈæŋkə ˌdeɪ/
the day of the week when remote workers are obliged to come into the office in order to connect with fellow workers and foster teamwork.
'Wednesday is our anchor day and we usually try to go for lunch together.'

a pat on the back (idiom)
approval, congratulations or praise for doing something really well.
'It looks like our offer has been accepted. The whole negotiating team deserves a pat on the back for making it happen.'

appraisal (noun) /əˈpreɪzəl/
an assessment of how someone or something is performing.
'We've got staff appraisals all week.'

'that's a big ask'

angel investor (noun)
/ˌeɪndʒəl ɪnˈvestə/
an individual who invests money into a small business in return for a percentage of ownership equity.
'We are currently looking for angel investors to help us get our business up and running.'

a numbers game (idiom)
a situation in which the key element is the quantity of something.
'This industry is a numbers game. The more you sell, the better you'll do.'

a seat at the table (idiom)
an active role in how decisions are made within a group.
'All women have been asking for is a seat at the table.'

ask (noun) /ɑːsk/
an informal request.
'I know it's a big ask, but could you help me set up the chairs for the meeting today?'

ask around (phrasal verb) /ˌɑːsk əˈraʊnd/
to ask more than one person in order to get information or assistance.
'I can ask around for you and see if anyone has any contacts in the media.'

a step in the right direction (phrase)
an action or development that will lead to positive progress.
'I think the changes we've made to the business are definitely a step in the right direction.'

a tall order (idiom)
if something is a tall order, it is very difficult to do or achieve.
'Persuading the team to take a pay freeze is going to be a tall order.'

at the end of the day (idiom)
used to state the most important thing that needs to be considered.
'Look, at the end of the day we need to reduce costs, and the only way to do that is by cutting our ad spend.'

at your earliest convenience (phrase)
a formal way of saying 'as soon as you have time'. It's mostly used in written English.
'Could you get the accounts to me at your earliest convenience?'

a walk in the park (idiom)
if something is a walk in the park, it is very easy.
'Building a website these days is a walk in the park compared to how it used to be.'

B

back (someone) (verb) /bæk/
to support something or someone.
'The board has backed the merger.'

back-and-forth (phrase)
discussion between two or more parties in which the exchange goes from one to the other.
'There's been a lot of back-and-forth between our respective lawyers.'

back office (noun) /ˈbæk ˌɒfɪs/
the administrative part of a business that supports the main business and is not customer-facing or client-facing.
'I work in the back office doing IT support.'

back-of-the-envelope (calculation/ number/maths) (phrase)
a quick mathematical calculation (also 'back-of-a-fag-packet').
'I've done some back-of-the-envelope maths and it looks like we are going to be over budget by ten thousand pounds.'

back-to-back (adjective) /ˌbæk tə ˈbæk/
consecutive, one after another, e.g. back-to-back interviews.
'I've had back-to-back meetings all morning.'

back to square one (idiom)
at the beginning of a plan again because your last attempt didn't work.
'Our proposal was rejected, so it looks like we are back to square one.'

back to the drawing board (idiom)
starting something again because the previous attempt was unsuccessful.
'These marketing ideas just aren't good enough, let's go back to the drawing board.'

bail out (phrasal verb) /ˌbeɪl ˈaʊt/
to help a person or organisation in financial trouble.
'The central bank is bailing out a lot of small businesses.'

ballpark figure (idiom)
an approximate quantity or figure.
'They've given us a ballpark figure for the office renovations and it's astronomical.'

bandwidth (noun) /ˈbændˌwɪdθ/
if you have the bandwidth to do something, you have the necessary time or mental ability.
'I'm afraid I haven't got the bandwidth to take on any more projects this month.'

base/basic salary (noun) /ˈbeɪs ˌsæləri/
the minimum amount you are paid for the hours you work.
'My base salary is thirty-two thousand pounds, but I get benefits and bonuses on top of that.'

be/get bogged down (phrasal verb) /ˌbɒgd ˈdaʊn/
if you get bogged down with something, you can't make progress with it.
'I'm getting bogged down with compliance requests, so I haven't been able to get started on the PPT.'

behind the curve (idiom)
less advanced and behind current ways of doing something.
'Our company is behind the curve when it comes to the adoption of AI technology.'

benchmarking (noun) /ˈbentʃˌmɑːkɪŋ/
the process of measuring your company's performance against a recognised standard.
'We believe benchmarking is an integral part of how we help companies grow.'

bend over backwards (idiom)
to make an extra special effort to do something.
'I'm bending over backwards to make things work between the new boss and me, but there's only so much I can do.'

best practice (noun) /ˌbest ˈpræktɪs/
a method of working that is widely recognised as the correct way of doing something.
'We've hired an HR expert to advise us on best practice for making redundancies.'

beta test (noun) /ˈbiːtə ˌtest/
an opportunity for real users to trial a new product before a full launch.
'Let's run a beta test on the new website features and see how they perform.'

between a rock and a hard place (idiom)
faced with two equally unappealing options.
'Does he report the mistake to his boss and risk losing his job, or does he keep quiet and worry that someone will find out? I feel like he's caught between a rock and a hard place!'

bigwig (noun) /ˈbɪgˌwɪg/
a person in a powerful position.
'All the bigwigs will be in the meeting this afternoon.'

bite off more than (one) can chew (idiom)
to attempt to do more than you are capable of.
'I'm worried Vijay has bitten off more than he can chew with this new project.'

bite the bullet (idiom)
to do something unpleasant or difficult that you don't want to do.
'At some stage we are going to have to bite the bullet and fire him.'

black hole (noun) /ˌblæk ˈhəʊl/
a product or business activity that costs a lot of money, but doesn't produce nearly as much income.
'Our online gaming platform is proving to be a massive black hole for the business.'

'bite the bullet'

blue-chip (adjective) /ˌbluːˈtʃɪp/
if you describe a company or investment as blue-chip, it has an excellent reputation and is considered very reliable.
'We only invest in blue-chip stocks.'

blue-sky thinking (phrase)
creative brainstorming for new ideas without limits or judgements.
'We need some blue-sky thinking if we are going to come up with an effective new advert.'

boil the ocean (idiom)
to try and do something that is overly ambitious and almost impossible.
'Keep the product simple! Let's not try to boil the ocean.'

'bonus'

bonus (noun) /ˈbəʊnəs/
an amount of money given to an individual or group as an incentive or reward.
'I'm hoping to get a sizeable bonus at the end of the financial year.'

boots on the ground (idiom)
people who are physically in a location working on something.
'Once we have boots on the ground in our Brazilian office, we'll be able to start ramping up production over there.'

bootstrap (verb) /ˈbuːtˌstræp/
to start or run a business with minimal money or resources.
'We bootstrapped this company for the first two years before investors came in.'

bottleneck (noun) /ˈbɒtəlˌnek/
an issue or problem that slows or stops progress.
'Since Brexit, we've had a number of bottlenecks when it comes to hiring staff from the EU.'

bottom-up (adjective) /ˌbɒtəmˈʌp/
starting with the lowest part of a hierarchy or process and working your way to the top.
'The company definitely has a bottom-up approach to decision-making.'

bounce around (phrasal verb) /ˌbaʊns əˈraʊnd/
to discuss an idea or topic, in an informal way, in order to get a variety of opinions.
'Let's sit down and bounce ideas around for the book launch.'

bounce rate (noun) /ˈbaʊns ˌreɪt/
the number of people who visit a website but leave after viewing just a single page.
'It's great to see our bounce rate has improved dramatically since the new website design.'

box-ticking (noun) /ˈbɒksˌtɪkɪŋ/
the process of doing something just to satisfy an administrative requirement, rather than it being useful in any way. (see also 'tick-box exercise').
'Doing this training course is such a box-ticking exercise. There's absolutely no need to do it.'

brainstorm (verb) /ˈbreɪnˌstɔːm/
to generate ideas and suggestions in a group.
'Let's brainstorm five ways we can diversify our revenue in the next 12 months.'

break even (phrase)
if a company breaks even, it doesn't lose money, but it doesn't make money either.
'We're looking to at least break even in our first year.'

breakout area (noun) /ˈbreɪkaʊt ˌeəriə/
an area for employees to eat, relax or hold informal meetings.
'The seventh floor has a very cool breakout area with a pool table and lots of comfy sofas.'

break the bank (idiom)
a humorously used phrase to say something is more expensive than you can afford.
'Getting some new mouse mats is hardly going to break the bank, is it?'

break the ice (idiom)
to do or say something to make everyone around you feel more comfortable.
'I've got a couple of activities to break the ice at my workshop today.'

bricks and mortar (noun) /ˌbrɪks ən ˈmɔːtə/
a business with a physical presence, as opposed to something online.
'After years of just selling online, we've finally decided to invest in some bricks and mortar in central London.'

bring forward (phrasal verb) /ˌbrɪŋ ˈfɔːwəd/
to change the time of a meeting or event so it happens earlier than previously planned.
'They've brought our meeting forward by an hour because the CFO needs to catch a plane.'

bring (something) to the table (idiom)
to make a useful contribution to an activity or make an offer in a negotiation.
'There are lots of qualities Simran brings to the table, especially her excellent presentation skills.'

bring (something) up (phrasal verb) /ˌbrɪŋ ˈʌp/
to raise a topic of conversation.
'Chiara brought up a really good point about holiday pay in our staff meeting.'

TOM'S TIPS

When learning phrasal verbs, it's important to know a few things. Firstly, there are two types of phrasal verbs: transitive and intransitive. Transitive phrasal verbs take an object, intransitive phrasal verbs don't.

Transitive – 'bring forward' – 'Let's bring the meeting forward.'
Intransitive – 'break down' – 'The photocopier has broken down.'

Transitive phrasal verbs can also be put in two categories: those that can be separated by an object and those that can't.

Separable – 'bail (somebody) out' / 'bail out (somebody)'
Inseparable – 'bogged down (in something)'

bullish (adjective) /ˈbʊlɪʃ/
confident and optimistic about the future of something.
'The CEO is very bullish about the state of the market right now.'

burn (oneself) out (phrasal verb) /ˌbɜːn ˈaʊt/
to make yourself unable to work and possibly unwell because you do too much work.
'I completely burned myself out in my twenties.'

burn rate (noun) /ˈbɜːn ˌreɪt/
the speed at which a new company spends its money. This usually comes in the early stages before it can generate a positive cash flow.
'Our burn rate is definitely slowing, but we are nowhere near becoming profitable.'

burn the candle at both ends (idiom)
to be very active and busy from early in the morning until late at night while not getting enough rest so that you become exhausted.
'It's been a mad week at work. I've been burning the candle at both ends.'

burn the midnight oil (idiom)
to stay up late working.
'I think we are all going to be burning the midnight oil tonight.'

business proposal (noun) /ˈbɪznɪs prəˌpəʊzəl/
a written document sent to a potential client in the hope of winning their business.
'We're just polishing off the business proposal now.'

busman's holiday (idiom)
an activity or time away from work where you actually do something related to your job.
'I spent a month teaching English to kids in the Philippines, which felt a bit like a busman's holiday.'

buy-in (noun) /ˈbaɪˌɪn/
support for a plan or idea.
'You'll need to get buy-in from the CTO if you want to implement those changes.'

by the book (idiom)
exactly according to the rules.
'I'm proud to say, we've always done things by the book at this taxi firm.'

'burn the midnight oil'

C

call it a day (phrase)
to decide that you are going to stop doing something, e.g. working.
'Let's call it a day everyone, and pick it up again tomorrow morning.'

call the shots (idiom)
if you call the shots, you are the person in a position of control to make decisions.
'We've all worked hard on this project, but ultimately it's our boss who calls the shots.'

can of worms (idiom)
a situation that seems simple but is much more complicated and difficult when you start to deal with it.
'The CEO's remarks have opened up a huge can of worms for the company and its shareholders.'

capacity (noun) /kəˈpæsəti/
the ability to do tasks or produce work. This can be affected by how much other work someone has or how much time they have.
A – 'Can you help with this PowerPoint?'
B – 'I'm afraid I don't have capacity right now. Can you ask someone else in the team?'

capital (noun) /ˈkæpɪtəl/
the amount of money an individual or business has available to start a business or grow its wealth.
'The amount of capital these giant tech firms have is extraordinary.'

carry coals to Newcastle (idiom)
to supply something to a place which already has a huge quantity of that thing and therefore doesn't need any more (also 'take coals to Newcastle').
'Trying to sell our semiconductor chips to Taiwanese car companies is like carrying coals to Newcastle.'

cascade (verb) /kæsˈkeɪd/
to pass information on to people. The information is usually passed down the company hierarchy from high to low.
'I'd like you to cascade the news down to your managers and they can inform their teams directly.'

cash cow (noun) /ˈkæʃ ˌkaʊ/
a product or service that steadily makes money over time.
'The iPhone has been a cash cow for Apple for years.'

cash flow (noun) /ˈkæʃ ˌfləʊ/
the movement of money in and out of a business.
'Would you like to borrow some money to help with cash flow right now?'

cash-strapped (adjective)
/ˈkæʃˌstræpt/
not having much money.
'Our department is a little cash-strapped at the moment so don't expect a pay rise anytime soon.'

TOM'S TIPS

You'll notice that a lot of phrases and idioms reference local life, e.g. 'carry coals to Newcastle' and 'have a finger in every pie'. I think it's always a good learning trick to find out what the equivalent is in your language. Is there an Italian or Spanish version of 'coals to Newcastle'? In Hindi or Korean, what would you say instead of 'a finger in every pie'?

These phrases offer us a great insight into local life and culture. For example, if you've been to the UK, you'll know that pies are a much-loved staple of British cuisine. Beef pies, chicken pies, veggie pies, mince pies. We love them all!

But why do we carry coals to Newcastle and not London or Birmingham? Well, the north-east of England used to be considered one of the great coal-mining regions in the UK. However, in the 1980s the pits were closed, meaning that one of the few things to live on from this proud industry is the phrase 'carry coals to Newcastle'.

catch-up (noun) /ˈkætʃˌʌp/
an informal meeting between people to find out what has happened since the last time they were in contact.
'Let's arrange a catch-up for when I get back from the conference.'

chair (verb) /tʃeə/
to preside over a meeting.
'Faisal is away today, so can you chair the meeting this afternoon?'

chase (somebody/something) up (phrasal verb) /ˌtʃeɪs ˈʌp/
to find out what is being done (by someone or about something).
'I still haven't heard from our lawyers. Can you chase them up for me?'

chaser (noun) /ˈtʃeɪsə/
a follow up email (also 'chaser email' or 'email chaser').
'I'll send a chaser email if they don't reply today.'

check in (with someone) (phrasal verb) /ˌtʃek ˈɪn/
to speak to or contact someone in order to get an update from them or see how they are.
'Arjun, make sure you check in with the interns in your team next week.'

chime in (phrasal verb) /ˌtʃaɪm ˈɪn/
to add your opinion or make a comment about something being discussed.
'Nick, do you want to chime in here and give us your sense of what's happening?'

chip in (with something) (phrasal verb) /ˌtʃɪp ˈɪn/
to add something to a conversation that is being had between other people or one in which you have minimal involvement.
'It was great to see the intern chip in with a few useful suggestions and ideas today.'

churn rate (noun) /ˈtʃɜːn ˌreɪt/
the number of customers that stop using a service at a point in time.
'The churn rate for our membership programme has been around 8% every month.'

circle back (to something) (phrasal verb) /ˌsɜːkəl ˈbæk/
to return to a topic, point, suggestion or idea.
'I'd like to circle back to what Kwan said about moving our operations abroad.'

clawback (noun) /ˈklɔːˌbæk/
a situation where a company takes back money it has already paid out.
'Recently there have been several clawbacks of bonuses paid to staff who were in breach of their contracts.'

client-facing (adjective) /ˈklaɪəntˌfeɪsɪŋ/
client-facing jobs or roles deal directly with people paying for their professional services.
'The project I'm on at the moment is client-facing, which has meant lots of travel in the last few months.'

close of play (idiom)
the end of the working day.
'Can you get the numbers to me by the close of play?'

co-create (verb) /ˌkəʊkriːˈeɪt/
to create something jointly with others.
'We've co-created this art exhibition with the British Arts Council.'

cog in the wheel (idiom)
a small part of a much larger business or organisation (also 'cog in the machine').
'I decided to join this startup because I didn't want to be just a cog in the wheel of some big tech firm.'

cold-call (verb) /ˌkəʊldˈkɔːl/
to call or visit a potential customer who has not previously expressed interest.
'I've spent the morning cold-calling people who might be interested in our new credit card offer.'

collaborate (verb) /kəˈlæbəˌreɪt/
to work with other people on a piece of work.
'Let's find a YouTuber to collaborate with on this campaign.'

'let's collaborate'

close a deal (phrase)
to accept and complete a business arrangement with another person or business.
'We just need to complete the paperwork and then we'll close the deal on Friday.'

come to a head (phrase)
to reach a point where action needs to be taken.
'Things came to a head in January when three of our senior staff resigned on the same day.'

compare apples and oranges (phrase)
used to say that there is no point comparing two things that are so different.
'Comparing some of the smaller regional offices with our London headquarters is like comparing apples and oranges.'

compassionate leave (noun) /kəmˌpæʃənət ˈliːv/
a period of absence from work given to an employee to help them deal with a tragic or sensitive personal issue, e.g. a bereavement.
'Nadine is going to lead the team meetings while Elijah is on compassionate leave.'

compensation (noun) /ˌkɒmpenˈseɪʃən/
a combination of an employee's salary plus bonuses, benefits and perks that are all paid to them. Often shortened to 'comp'.
'They offered me a very generous compensation package.'

compliance (noun) /kəmˈplaɪəns/
the department that makes sure a company adheres to laws and regulations.
'I'd check with compliance before going ahead with that deal.'

conference call (noun) /ˈkɒnfrəns ˌkɔːl/
a work-related phone or video call involving multiple participants.
'We've got a conference call with the clients scheduled for tomorrow at 3 p.m.'

conflict of interest (phrase)
a situation in which personal interests could potentially cause bias in decision-making.
'My brother-in-law works for the defendant's law firm so I need to declare a conflict of interest.'

consensus (noun) /kənˈsensəs/
general agreement among a group of people.
'If the team can reach a consensus, we'll be able to go ahead with the recruitment drive.'

contractor (noun) /kənˈtræktə/
an individual or company that is paid by another company to complete a specific project.
'We've got a couple of the building contractors coming in today to look at the roof.'

core business (noun) /ˌkɔː ˈbɪznɪs/
the business activity that is the most important to a company and drives the majority of their profits.
'While it's important to diversify, we mustn't forget that buying and selling properties is our core business.'

core competency (noun) /ˌkɔː ˈkɒmpɪtənsi/
an essential skill that is required to do a job or activity.
'A working knowledge of Adobe InDesign is one of the core competencies for this role.'

corner the market (idiom)
if a business corners the market, it has great success selling a service or product and is more successful than any other business.
'There was a time when Tesla had really cornered the EV market.'

corporate ladder (phrase)
the hierarchy of jobs within a company from the most junior to the most senior. Common collocations include moving up or climbing the corporate ladder.
'If you want to climb the corporate ladder, you need to work harder than everyone else in this company.'

co-worker (noun) /ˈkəʊˌwɜːkə/
someone you work with (synonym of 'colleague').
'Sam and I were co-workers at the BBC.'

co-working (noun) /ˈkəʊˌwɜːkɪŋ/
the use of a space as a working environment by people who are self-employed, freelance or from different companies. It is often done with the aim of helping to create community and encourage knowledge sharing.
'Co-working has really helped me find a group of like-minded people who I can bounce ideas off.'

co-working space (noun)
/ˈkəʊwɜːkɪŋ ˌspeɪs/
a physical location in which co-working takes place.
'WeWork was one of the first co-working spaces to open up in London.'

cross that bridge when you (get/come) to it (idiom)
used to say that you will deal with a future problem if or when it happens.
'We're going to need a bigger office soon, but let's cross that bridge when we get to it.'

crowdfunding (noun) /ˈkraʊdˌfʌndɪŋ/
when a large number of people give a small amount of money in order to help pay for a project.
'With the help of crowdfunding we managed to raise sixty thousand pounds to pay for a new community event space.'

crunch the numbers (idiom)
to perform detailed mathematical calculations.
'We need to crunch the numbers before we make any more hiring decisions.'

crush it (phrase)
an informal way to say perform excellently.
'Team, you are crushing it! Keep up the good work.'

C-suite (noun) /ˈsiːˌswiːt/
the group of people who have 'chief' at the beginning of their job title and are therefore seen as having the most important jobs in a company.
'It's time we saw more diversity in our C-suite.'

'Co-working spaces have become hugely popular in the UK, particularly in larger urban areas. Not only do they offer great places to work, but they also include networking events, useful amenities and a sense of community.'
Teacher Tom

curveball (noun) /ˈkɜːvˌbɔːl/
something surprising or unexpected that is potentially difficult to deal with.
'These travel strikes are a bit of a curveball. Do you think everyone will be able to get into the office?'

customer-facing (adjective) /ˈkʌstəməˌfeɪsɪŋ/
having direct interactions with customers.
'I would prefer a customer-facing role because I love meeting new people.'

'cut to the chase'

customer journey (noun) /ˈkʌstəmə ˌdʒɜːni/
all the interactions and experiences a customer has with your company or brand when making a purchase.
'We need to focus on ways to improve the customer journey.'

cut corners (idiom)
to do something less well than you could in order to save money or time.
'Our previous manager used to cut corners all the time, but now things are much more thorough and professional.'

cut (it/things) fine (idiom)
to allow very little time to do something.
'We could leave the decision until Friday, but we'd be cutting it fine.'

cut-throat (adjective) /ˈkʌtˌθrəʊt/
very competitive and ruthless.
'I knew going into it that fashion was a very cut-throat industry.'

cut to the chase (idiom)
to get to the point without wasting time.
'Can we cut to the chase and discuss what's really going on with the company's finances.'

D

data-driven (adjective) /ˈdeɪtəˌdrɪvən/
if something is data-driven, it is based on information and analysis.
'We need to make some data-driven decisions about how this department is going to move forward.'

dead-end job (noun) /ˌdedend ˈdʒɒb/
a job with no future prospects.
'I spent all of my twenties going from one dead-end job to another.'

deadline (noun) /ˈdedˌlaɪn/
the point in time by which something must be completed.
'I've got a few tight deadlines, so I think I'm going to be working all weekend.'

dead wood (noun) /ˌded ˈwʊd/
someone or something that is no longer useful or necessary.
'The first thing I did as CEO was identify the dead wood in the company.'

deck (noun) /dek/
a set of slides.
'Can you get started on the presentation deck while I collate the last bits of data?'

deep dive (noun) /ˌdiːp ˈdaɪv/
a detailed analysis of something.
'I've asked Miguel and his team to do a deep dive into our big competitors in the Spanish market.'

deets (noun) /diːts/
a very informal form of 'details'.
'Has anyone got the deets for the networking event tonight?'

delegate (verb) /ˈdelɪˌgeɪt/
to choose someone to do a duty, job or task.
'I've delegated organising the Christmas party to Raj and his team, as they did such a good job last year.'

deleverage (verb) /diːˈlevərɪdʒ/
to reduce the amount of debt a business has.
'The business is in a position to deleverage after a few years of massive growth.'

deliverable (noun) /dɪˈlɪvərəbəl/
something that needs to be provided at the completion of a project, e.g. a report, a product, a service.
'Do you think we are going to be able to hit all our deliverables on this project?'

digital nomad (noun) /ˌdɪdʒɪtəl ˈnəʊmæd/
a person who is able to earn money working online while living in different locations around the world, rather than staying in one fixed place.
'My dream is to quit my job as a bar manager and become a digital nomad.'

'digital nomad'

digital transformation (noun)
/ˌdɪdʒɪtəl trænsfəˈmeɪʃən/
the integration of digital technology to improve or change the systems within a business.
'We are undergoing a huge digital transformation right now that will help us compete on a global level.'

direct report (noun) /daɪˌrekt rɪˈpɔːt/
if someone is your direct report, you manage them and take responsibility for their performance.
'I've set up informal meetings with my direct reports this week to check in on them.'

disruptive (adjective) /dɪsˈrʌptɪv/
changing and reimagining how an industry operates by doing things in new ways.
'There's been so much disruptive innovation in our industry over the last five years.'

diversify (verb) /daɪˈvɜːsɪˌfaɪ/
to increase the variety of something, e.g. investments, products or services.
'Disney diversified their revenue streams when they created Disney Plus.'

done and dusted (idiom)
finished and complete.
'We just need to get the CEO's signature and then the deal is done and dusted.'

dot the i's and cross the t's (idiom)
to make sure all the details are correct before finishing something like a task or project.
'We just need to dot the i's and cross the t's on the contract and then we are ready to complete the deal.'

double-check (verb) /ˌdʌbəlˈtʃek/
to check something for a second time to make sure it's all correct, accurate or safe.
'Double-check your calculations before sending your spreadsheet to HR.'

double down (on something) (phrasal verb) /ˌdʌbəl ˈdaʊn/
to commit with even more determination to a position already taken.
'The company has really doubled down on its belief that South America will be the biggest market in 20 years time.'

double-edged sword (idiom)
a situation which has two sides to it, one positive and one negative (also 'two-edged sword').
'Honestly, this job is proving to be a bit of a double-edged sword. I'm getting more money, but I spend most of my life in the office.'

downshifting (noun) /ˈdaʊnˌʃɪftɪŋ/
the act of reducing your work commitments in order to have more time to yourself.
'My partner and I have been talking about downshifting and moving to the countryside for years.'

TOM'S TIPS

Proficient speakers of English use connected speech to join words and sounds together. It helps us sound more fluent! Let's take 'done and dusted' as an example. There's a weak form on 'and' so it's pronounced /ən/. We'd also link it to 'done', so it would be said /ˌdʌnən ˈdʌstɪd/.

'drop the ball'

downsize (verb) /ˈdaʊnˌsaɪz/
to reduce the size of a business or organisation.
'The agency has had to downsize significantly since the pandemic.'

down the road/line (idiom)
in the future.
'Down the road, we'd like to expand our business into Asia.'

downtime (noun) /ˈdaʊnˌtaɪm/
time to relax.
'Make sure you get some downtime this weekend everyone; you've earned it.'

draw (something) up (phrasal verb) /ˌdrɔː ˈʌp/
to prepare something official in writing.
'We'll be in touch once the lawyers have drawn up your contract.'

drill down (phrasal verb) /ˌdrɪl ˈdaʊn/
to examine something in great detail.
'I'm going to spend this afternoon drilling down into the numbers for our last quarter.'

drive a hard bargain (idiom)
to negotiate in a very determined way in order to get the deal you want.
'Her agent drove a very hard bargain, but eventually we came to an agreement.'

drop the ball (idiom)
to make a mistake or miss an opportunity.
'The government really dropped the ball with their mini-budget. It almost crashed the economy!'

due diligence (noun) /ˌdjuː ˈdɪlɪdʒəns/
careful examination of a person or company before entering into a business relationship with them.
'Let's make sure we do our due diligence before making an offer for this company.'

E

early adopter (noun) /ˌɜːli əˈdɒptə/
one of the first people to start using a new product or service.
'Apple has a loyal army of early adopters.'

emerging market (noun)
/ɪˌmɜːdʒɪŋ ˈmɑːkɪt/
the market of a developing country that is growing, but is not yet at the level of a developed nation.
'We are allocating a lot of our capital into emerging markets as we seek to find new growth areas.'

end-to-end (adjective) /ˌendtuːˈend/
from the very beginning of a process to the end.
'We provide end-to-end solutions for companies launching new products in the Chinese market.'

'entrepreneur'

elephant in the room (idiom)
a big problem or controversial issue that is evident to everyone but is not spoken about.
'Clearly the elephant in the room is the CFO's dismissal today, but maybe we address that in another meeting.'

elevator pitch (noun) /ˈelɪveɪtə ˌpɪtʃ/
a succinct explanation of something, e.g. a new business or product. It's designed to persuade someone to invest or become involved.
'After years of practice, I've got the elevator pitch for my software company down to four minutes.'

eleventh hour (noun) /ɪˌlevənθ ˈaʊə/
the very last moment that something is possible.
'We didn't think the sale would go through and then at the eleventh hour new investors came in and the deal was done.'

end user (noun) /ˈend ˌjuːzə/
the individual who is ultimately going to use a product or service.
'In product design, we never lose sight of who the end user is and what they want.'

entrepreneur (noun) /ˌɒntrəprəˈnɜː/
someone who starts a business.
'I don't think my risk tolerance is high enough to become an entrepreneur.'

entry-level (adjective) /ˈentriˌlevəl/
at the lowest level of a company's hierarchy.
'Our entry-level salaries are very competitive compared to other banks.'

escalate (something) (verb) /ˈeskəˌleɪt/
if you escalate a complaint, problem or serious issue, you involve someone more senior in order to help.
'This is the third time he's been rude to a colleague. I think we need to escalate this to his line manager.'

executive decision (noun) /ɪɡˌzekjətɪv dɪˈsɪʒən/
a decision taken unilaterally, i.e. by one individual or company.
'Because of the storm, I've taken the executive decision to close the shop today. You can all go home.'

exit interview (noun) /ˈeksɪt ˌɪntəvjuː/
an interview an employer conducts with an employee who is leaving the company.
'Let's set up an exit interview for Sophie before she leaves on Friday.'

exit strategy (noun) /ˈeksɪt ˌstrætədʒi/
a plan for how someone is going to leave or sell a company.
'Have you got an exit strategy for your start- up?'

expedite (verb) /ˈekspəˌdaɪt/
to make something happen faster.
'The packages have been expedited to the US so we get them there before Thanksgiving.'

expense (verb) /ɪkˈspens/
to charge a payment as an expense.
'When I'm on a work trip, I always expense my lunches and dinners.'

expenses (noun) /ɪkˈspensɪz/
the money spent while performing your job that is usually paid back to you by your employer, e.g. food or transport costs.
'Have you claimed your expenses for the Manchester trip?'

F

face time (noun) /ˈfeɪs ˌtaɪm/
time spent in-person with people rather than over email or text.
'I really want our new recruits to get as much face time in the office as possible.'

facilitate (verb) /fəˈsɪlɪˌteɪt/
to help make something happen more easily.
'Can you stay late to facilitate the client meeting?'

fall through the cracks (idiom)
if an important detail falls through the cracks, it is missed or overlooked (also 'slip through the cracks').
'Can everyone double-check that we haven't let any details of this deal fall through the cracks?'

feed back (phrasal verb) /ˌfiːd ˈbæk/
to report back to someone on the results of a meeting, discussion, interview or research.
'If you could spend five minutes feeding back what the client said to you, that would be great.'

feedback (noun) /ˈfiːdˌbæk/
comments on how someone or something has performed. Whether positive or negative, its purpose is to help learn and improve.
'I'd love to get some feedback on how you think I've done in my first two weeks here.'

file for (something) (phrasal verb) /ˈfaɪl ˌfɔː/
to make an official request to a court for something, e.g. bankruptcy.
'Sadly, lots of companies had to file for bankruptcy during the pandemic.'

financial year (noun) /faɪˌnænʃəl ˈjɪə/
a 12-month period in which an organisation calculates its budgets and accounts (not necessarily January to December).
'We are going to have to tighten our belts in the next financial year.'

'Have you noticed how many of our expressions are related to parts of the body? We've got "face time" and "finger-pointing" in this section, but other examples include "play it by ear", "heads up" and "word of mouth", to name but a few.'

Teacher Tom

'flesh out the details'

finger-pointing (noun) /ˈfɪŋgəˌpɔɪntɪŋ/
the act of blaming someone for something going wrong.
'There was a lot of finger-pointing after the disastrous product launch.'

fire (someone) (verb) /faɪə/
to terminate someone's employment.
'Have you ever had to fire anyone?'

firefighting (noun) /ˈfaɪəˌfaɪtɪŋ/
dealing with urgent problems as they arise rather than working in a planned manner.
'I've spent the whole morning firefighting to keep this deal alive.'

firm (something) up (phrasal verb) /ˌfɜːm ˈʌp/
to make a plan or decision more definite and certain to happen.
'Perhaps in the meeting we can firm up the dates for the conference.'

first pass (noun) /ˌfɜːst ˈpɑːs/
the first draft of something, e.g. a document, memo or presentation.
'I've attached my first pass at the Q1 budget if you'd like to take a look.'

fit for purpose (adjective) /ˌfɪt fə ˈpɜːpəs/
if something is fit for purpose, it is capable of doing exactly what it needs to do.
'We need to redraft these legal documents, as they aren't fit for purpose at the moment.'

fit interview (noun) /ˈfɪt ˌɪntəvjuː/
an interview that seeks to determine if the candidate suits the culture of the company (also known as a 'culture fit interview').
'I think she'd be a great hire. She absolutely aced the fit interview.'

fixed costs (noun) /ˌfɪkst ˈkɒsts/
the costs a business has to pay regardless of performance, e.g. electricity, rent and salaries.
'One way to reduce our fixed costs would be to downsize to a smaller office space.'

flag (something) (verb) /flæg/
to draw someone's attention to a problem or something important (also 'flag something up').
'I just want to flag the possibility that half the team might be on a training day next week.'

flesh out (something) (phrasal verb) /ˌfleʃ ˈaʊt/
to add more information to something.
'I've sent the business plan to Ben and Panos so they can flesh out the details.'

flip-flop (verb) /ˈflɪpˌflɒp/
to switch from one opinion to another, usually to the annoyance of others.
'At the last minute, my boss flip-flopped on her decision to ask everyone to work on Saturday so now we are all going in.'

'food for thought'

float (something) (verb) /fləʊt/
to suggest a plan or idea.
'Michelle has floated the idea of our team having a weekly social.'

float (something) to the top of (someone's) inbox (phrase)
a phrase used in an email to bring someone's attention to important information contained in a previous email you've sent, but hasn't been replied to.
'Hi Connor, I'm just floating this email to the top of your inbox in case you missed my question about your annual leave request.'

fly (verb) /flaɪ/
if an idea or suggestion flies, it is successful or accepted.
'I'm not sure that suggestion is going to fly with the team, but we can try.'

fly in the ointment (idiom)
a small singular thing that spoils the success or enjoyment of everything else.
'We've got a fabulous training day planned. The only potential fly in the ointment is the threat of rail strikes.'

follow (something) up (phrasal verb) /ˌfɒləʊ ˈʌp/
to find out how something has progressed.
'Let's give it a week and then you can follow up with their analyst and see how the investment has performed.'

food for thought (idiom)
something to think carefully about.
'The new offer they've made me is definitely food for thought.'

for the foreseeable future (phrase)
for as long into the future as you can imagine (also 'in the foreseeable future').
'I can't see us moving offices for the foreseeable future.'

forward planning (noun) /ˌfɔːwəd ˈplænɪŋ/
the process of making plans that consider what might happen in the future.
'The team has been doing a lot of forward planning to model out what the next five years look like for us.'

forward-thinking (adjective) /ˌfɔːwədˈθɪŋkɪŋ/
looking to the future and planning for it.
'She's one of the most forward-thinking designers in her profession.'

framework (noun) /ˈfreɪmˌwɜːk/
a set of principles, best practices and ideas that provides a structure to operate within.
'We need to set up a legal framework for how we expand the business outside of the UK.'

freelance (adjective) /ˈfriːˌlɑːns/
if you do freelance work, you are not employed permanently by any one company. Instead, you do pieces of work for more than one company.
'I started my career as a freelance journalist working in South Africa.'

TOM'S TIPS

Many of our Business English phrases actually have their origins in American English. One example is 'furlough', which only really entered our wider lexicon during the pandemic. Other useful American phrases we commonly use have their origins in sport. For example, 'ballpark figure' and 'step up to the plate' come from baseball, and 'throw in the towel' is a term often used in boxing. Keep an eye out for more of them as you go through this A–Z section of the book.

freelancer (noun) /ˈfriːˌlɑːnsə/
someone who isn't permanently employed by one company but instead does work for a variety of them.
'One of the hardest things about being a freelancer is the uncertainty of not knowing when the next job will come.'

from scratch (idiom)
from the beginning, starting from zero.
'My grandmother started this company from scratch, just after the war ended.'

from the ground up (idiom)
completely from the bottom to the top.
'The culture of this company needs to change from the ground up.'

front-load (something) (verb) /ˈfrʌntˌləʊd/
to put a larger amount of resources at the beginning of a process.
'We've front-loaded the advertising campaign so that it can generate a lot of interest in a short period of time.'

front office (noun) /ˌfrʌnt ˈɒfɪs/
the part of a business where staff interact directly with the customers.
'I've worked in the front office for almost 20 years now.'

full steam ahead (idiom)
progressing with speed and energy.
'Now we've got the contract signed, it's full steam ahead until November.'

furlough (noun) /ˈfɜːləʊ/
if a worker is put on furlough, they are asked not to work, but continue to be employed and receive a percentage of their salary. It is an American term that was adopted during the Covid-19 pandemic by many UK companies.
'My company was one of the first to put everyone on furlough when the pandemic hit.'

G

game plan (noun) /ˈgeɪm ˌplæn/
a strategy for success.
'We need to double our revenue in the next six months. What's the game plan?'

gardening leave (noun) /ˈgɑːdənɪŋ ˌliːv/
a period of time after someone leaves a job, when they are still paid by the employer but can't work or start a new job.
'Have you heard Jasmine has been put on gardening leave?'

gauge (verb) /geɪdʒ/
to assess or make a judgement on something, e.g. how people feel about something.
'It's hard to gauge how the client feels about the new branding.'

GBP (noun) /ˌdʒiːbiːˈpiː/
abbreviation for British Pound.
'GBP is now weaker against USD than it was this time last year.'

get (something) across (phrasal verb) /ˌget əˈkrɒs/
to make an idea or concept understood.
'It's important we get our message across that we really value their hard work and effort on this project.'

get a read on (something) (phrase)
to get an opinion or position on a topic.
'Can I get your read on this email I've just received?'

get back to (someone) (phrasal verb) /ˌget ˈbæk tuː/
to speak to someone at a later time in order to give them an answer or some information.
'Can I get back to you this afternoon with the draft?'

get down to business (idiom)
to start discussing or doing the thing you need to do.
'Let's get down to business and finalise the dates for the product launch.'

get (one's) ducks in a row (idiom)
to have everything organised and planned ahead of time (also 'have (one's) ducks in a row').
'Let's make sure we've got all our ducks in a row before our meeting with the legal team tomorrow.'

get (one's) foot in the door (idiom)
to get an opportunity with an organisation at a low level. The hope is that once you are in, you will be successful in the future.
'She just needs to get her foot in the door at one of these big TV companies then I'm sure she'll do really good things.

'game plan'

‘get the ball rolling’

get (one’s) head down (idiom)
to be completely focused and work hard on a specific task.
‘I need to finish this report so I’m going to get my head down for a few hours.’

get (something) off the ground (idiom)
to start something like a business or a plan, usually involving lots of hard work.
‘In my career, I’ve managed to get three startups off the ground, but starting an NGO is a whole different challenge.’

get (something) over the line (idiom)
to finally complete a task or deal.
‘Things will settle down once we get this deal over the line.’

get sidetracked (phrase)
to be distracted or have your attention diverted away from what you should be doing.
‘Sorry I got completely sidetracked! I’ll get the presentation to you in an hour.’

get the ball rolling (idiom)
to start something or begin to make it happen.
‘We need to get the ball rolling on this campaign as soon as possible.’

get the hang of (something) (idiom)
to begin to realise how to do something, e.g. a new skill.
‘Just when I’d got the hang of using Teams, they switched us over to Slack.’

get the wrong end of the stick (idiom)
to completely misunderstand something.
‘Are you saying we need to start all over again, or have I got the wrong end of the stick?’

get (one’s) wires crossed (idiom)
if two or more people get their wires crossed, they understand or interpret a situation in different ways.
‘I’m so sorry! I thought you were going to do it. I think we must have got our wires crossed.’

gig economy (noun) /ˈɡɪɡ ɪˌkɒnəmi/
a labour market in which jobs are on temporary short-term contracts.
‘The growing gig economy has changed the way people work in this part of the world.’

give (someone) a hand (idiom)
to help someone.
‘Can I give you a hand with anything, Arjun?’

TOM'S TIPS

In spontaneous speech, proficient English speakers add an intrusive /w/ sound when one word ends with /əʊ/ and the next word begins with a vowel. It helps blend the words together.

'go over . . .' = /gəʊ wəʊvə/

'go out of . . .' = /gəʊ waʊ təv/

'go into . . .' = /gəʊ wɪntuː/

give a hundred per cent (idiom)
to do something with all your effort (also 'give a hundred and ten per cent').
'Everyone needs to give a hundred per cent in these next few weeks as we lead up to the launch.'

give (someone) a steer (phrase)
to give someone advice or guidance to help them do a task.
'My boss has asked me to write this proposal. Can you give me a steer?'

give (someone) notice (phrase)
if you give someone their notice, you tell them to leave their job after a period of time.
'The company I work for are making loads of redundancies and they gave us all two weeks' notice.'

give the green light (idiom)
to give official permission or approval to do something. Think traffic lights: green means go!
'We've been given the green light to go ahead with the merger.'

give (something/someone) the OK (phrase)
to give someone permission to do something.
'I'm just waiting for someone to give me the OK before I send out this email.'

glass ceiling (noun) /ˌɡlɑːs ˈsiːlɪŋ/
a metaphor used to describe the invisible barriers placed in the way of women and minority groups in the workplace.
'It's time we smashed through the glass ceiling and took our seats at the top table of this organisation.'

go above and beyond (idiom)
to put in extra effort so that you exceed the expectations of others.
'I can't recommend this agency highly enough, they've gone completely above and beyond.'

go a long way towards (doing something) (idiom)
to be very helpful in achieving something.
'Signing this huge contract will go a long way towards helping us stay in business for another year.'

go (around) in circles (idiom)
to keep returning to the same topic, problem or issue without making any progress.
'Discussions about where to open another retail location have been going around in circles, so we've decided to come back to it after the weekend.'

going forward (phrase)
in the future.
'Going forward, we should really try to schedule daily meetings.'

go into administration (phrase)
if a company goes into administration, it is in a legal process in which the direct running of the company goes to administrators appointed by the court. This is usually because it has become insolvent and cannot pay its debts.
'They are doing everything they can to make sure the company doesn't go into administration.'

golden handcuffs (noun) /ˌɡəʊldən ˈhændkʌfs/
a generous amount of money offered by a company to a senior employee in order to persuade them to remain at the company and not work somewhere else.
'I'd love to get to the stage in my career when I'm offered golden handcuffs to continue working here.'

good to go (phrase)
ready or prepared for something.
'The presentation is good to go.'

go out of (one's) way (idiom)
to make a special effort to help someone, even if it inconveniences you.
'Isabella is amazing! She always goes out of her way to help her colleagues.'

go over (someone's) head (about something) (idiom)
to bypass someone who is directly above you and go straight to someone more powerful in order to get what you want.
'If my boss won't let me work from home twice a week, I'm going to have to go over her head.'

go public (phrase)
to go from being a private company to a public company.
'Oatly, the oat milk company, went public a few years ago.'

go the extra mile (idiom)
to make an added effort to achieve something.
'It's great to see interns going the extra mile to prove they deserve a full-time job.'

'go the extra mile'

go through the floor (idiom)
if prices or figures go through the floor, they drop to very low levels quickly.
'House prices in this area have gone through the floor since the pandemic.'

go through the roof (idiom)
if prices or figures go through the roof, they increase very rapidly.
'The price of copper has gone through the roof in the last six months.'

go to the wall (idiom)
to go out of business or fail.
'I was really sad when our local ice-cream shop went to the wall. It was a huge part of my childhood.'

go under (idiom)
to go out of business or fail.
'Sadly, it looks like his business is about to go under.'

'graduate scheme'

graduate scheme/programme (noun) /ˈgrædʒuət ˌskiːm/
an entry-level job for newly graduated university students that also acts as a training programme for them to learn about the business (also 'grad scheme').
'I've been accepted onto the Barclays graduate scheme.'

gross misconduct (noun) /ˌgrəʊs mɪsˈkɒndʌkt/
when an employee seriously violates the rules of their contract, e.g. by committing theft or fraud.
'Did you hear they fired the HR lead for gross misconduct?'

growth hacking (noun) /ˈgrəʊθ ˌhækɪŋ/
the process of rapidly experimenting with different strategies to achieve huge growth within a business.
'Growth hacking has been instrumental in helping us gain thousands more customers, almost overnight.'

H

hand in (one's) notice (phrase)
to inform your employer that you are going to leave your job, usually after a period of time.
'It feels so good to have handed in my notice at work. I'm free!'

handover (noun) /ˈhændəʊvə/
the act of passing responsibility or control on to someone else.
'It's our job to make sure the leadership handover goes smoothly.'

hand (something) over (phrasal verb) /ˌhænd ˈəʊvə/
to pass responsibility for something on to someone else.
'Before you go on leave, make sure you hand over any tasks you want me to do.'

hand over fist (idiom)
at a fast rate.
'Since he started the agency they have been losing money hand over fist.'

hands are tied (idiom)
if someone's hands are tied, they can't do what they want to do because of rules or restrictions placed upon them.
'I'd love to give you the day off, but my hands are tied.'

hard skills (noun) /ˈhɑːd ˌskɪlz/
the tangible technical skills gained through training and work experience.
'It's really important to develop a wide set of hard skills like coding and PowerPoint.'

hard stop (noun) /ˈhɑːd ˌstɒp/
a definite time that someone has to finish or leave a meeting.
'I'm happy to jump on a call now, but I've got a hard stop at 3:30 p.m.'

have a finger in every pie (idiom)
to be involved in multiple activities at the same time.
'Taylor is the person to call. She seems to have a finger in every pie over there at Meta.'

'have a finger in every pie'

TOM'S TIPS

Make sure you learn where to put the stress on words. All nouns, verbs, phrasal verbs and adjectives have primary stress marked with ˈ and any secondary stress marked with ˌ in the phonetic script, e.g. 'headhunter' /ˈhedˌhʌntə/. This shows you that the main stress or emphasis is on the first syllable, and there is a secondary stress, which is weaker than primary stress but stronger than no stress at all, on the second syllable. Compare this with 'facilitate' /fəˈsɪlɪˌteɪt/, where the main stress is on the second syllable, and there is a secondary stress on the last syllable.

have a lot of plates spinning (idiom)
to have a number of different tasks to do at the same time.
'Today has been a bit hectic. I've got a lot of plates spinning at the moment.'

have (a lot/too much) on (one's) plate (idiom)
to have too many tasks or activities to do.
'If you've got too much on your plate, let me know and I'll help you out.'

have a word with (someone) (phrase)
to have a short conversation.
'Can I have a quick word with you in my office?'

have (bigger/other) fish to fry (idiom)
to have something more important to do.
'Don't waste your time with these micro influencers, we've got bigger fish to fry.'

have irons in the fire (idiom)
to be involved in several activities or plans at the same time.
'I'd like to keep working here, but I've got a few irons in the fire in case it doesn't work out.'

have legs (idiom)
a way to describe an idea, plan or activity that has the potential to succeed or continue.
'I really think this idea has legs, we just need to flesh out the details.'

have skin in the game (idiom)
to have a vested interest in something's success or failure, often financial involvement.
'The only way to learn about investing is to have skin in the game.'

have (one's) work cut out (idiom)
to do something that is very difficult.
'The new CEO has her work cut out making this business profitable.'

headhunter (noun) /ˈhedˌhʌntə/
someone who works in recruitment and identifies the best candidates for a job.
'A headhunter contacted me on LinkedIn to see if I'd be interested in applying for a senior PR job.'

head (something) up (phrasal verb) /ˌhed ˈʌp/
to take charge or lead something, e.g. a project, department or business.
'Imani heads up the European marketing team.'

heads-up (noun) /ˈhedzˌʌp/
if you give someone a heads-up, you tell them something is going to happen so they can prepare for it.
'Just a heads-up, everyone, that the owner and her family are coming into the office today.'

headwinds (noun) /ˈhedˌwɪndz/
factors that slow down progress or affect a business negatively.
'We've seen a number of economic headwinds impact our sales this year.'

heavy lifting (noun) /ˌhevi ˈlɪftɪŋ/
if you do the heavy lifting, you do the majority of a task and often the most difficult parts of it too.
'Our US team is doing the heavy lifting on this, but we'll assist them where we can.'

hedge (one's) bets (idiom)
to reduce your risk by leaving yourself with more than one option for success.
'I'm hedging my bets and speaking to three recruiters.'

helicopter view (noun) /helɪˌkɒptə ˈvjuː/
a general view rather than a detailed one.
'Give us the helicopter view of how the East Asian market is looking.'

hit the ground running (idiom)
to begin an activity immediately and with all your enthusiasm.
'I start my new job in January and I really want to hit the ground running.'

hit the nail on the head (idiom)
to say something that is exactly right.
'Warren Buffet hit the nail on the head when he said "It takes 20 years to build a reputation and 5 minutes to ruin it".'

hold (someone's) feet to the fire (idiom)
to pressure someone into doing something or hold them responsible until they comply.
'The company has made environmental promises in the past and now it's time for us to hold their feet to the fire.'

hold the fort (idiom)
to take responsibility for something while the person normally responsible is away.
'Thanks for holding the fort while I was away.'

'hit the nail on the head'

'hybrid working'

hold the pen (idiom)
if you are holding the pen on a task, you are the primary person responsible for it.
'Ultimately, I'm the one holding the pen on this so it's imperative we get it right.'

hold (someone) to account (phrase)
to make someone take responsibility and explain their actions (also 'hold (someone) accountable').
'The CTO must be held to account for the ongoing tech issues.'

hot-desking (noun) /ˌhɒtˈdeskɪŋ/
a way of working in which there are no assigned desks so anyone can sit anywhere.
'This floor is all hot-desking, so feel free to sit anywhere.'

housekeeping (noun) /ˈhaʊsˌkiːpɪŋ/
used in meetings to refer to the general activities and tasks that are involved in daily working life.
'Just a little bit of housekeeping before we start. Mary and Asma are going to be the fire wardens this month, so please follow their instructions in the event of an emergency.'

how long is a piece of string? (idiom)
a phrase that is used to answer a question where the answer could be anything.
A – 'Do you know how many people can use this service at the same time?'
B – 'How long is a piece of string?'

hybrid working (noun) /ˌhaɪbrɪd ˈwɜːkɪŋ/
a way of working that consists of spending part of the week in the office and the rest of the time working remotely.
'We've had a hybrid-working model for the last two years and it's proving to be really popular with our staff.'

I

I don't see why not (phrase)
a way of saying 'yes' when someone asks for permission to do something.
A – 'Would it be OK if I skipped the meeting this afternoon? I've got a dental appointment.'
B – 'I don't see why not.'

impactful (adjective) /ɪmˈpæktfəl/
having a powerful effect.
'Moving the call centres offshore has been really impactful on our profit margins.'

in a nutshell (idiom)
used to say that you are giving only the most important points in the most concise way possible.
'Don't worry if you didn't hear the full speech. In a nutshell, the leadership team thinks we've outperformed our competitors because of our new marketing strategy.'

indispensable (adjective) /ˌɪndɪˈspensəbəl/
if someone or something is indispensable, they are critically important and you can't do without them.
'Yotam and Jackson are indispensable members of my team. I don't know what I'd do if either of them left.'

in hot water (idiom)
in trouble because of something you've said or done.
'The CFO is in hot water because of some controversial posts he sent out on Friday.'

in-house (adjective) /ˌɪnˈhaʊs/
describes activities or work done internally within a company.
'The in-house magazine we produce is actually a great read.'

in lieu (of) (idiom) /ɪn ˈljuː/
instead (of).
'If you work this Saturday, you can claim a day off in lieu.'

in on the ground floor (idiom)
involved in something from the beginning.
'I'm so envious of all those people who got in on the ground floor of Google and Amazon.'

in the bag (idiom)
used when you know something will happen for certain.
'The Adidas contract is in the bag. I spoke to their MD today and she confirmed it.'

in the black (idiom)
in credit (not in debt).
'The accounts are in the black for the first time since the pandemic.'

'in the bag'

in the dark (about something) (idiom)
if you are in the dark about something, you don't know anything about it, often because people are choosing not to tell you.
'The whole team has been left completely in the dark about this proposed acquisition.'

in the driver's seat (idiom)
in charge or in control of a situation.
'If you know you're the candidate they really want, then you're in the driver's seat – you could negotiate a higher salary.'

in the loop (idiom)
informed about news or information that is shared between a closed group of people (see also 'out of the loop').
'Keep me in the loop and let me know if there are any changes to the itinerary.'

in the nick of time (idiom)
only just before something needs to happen.
'We filed the report in the nick of time.'

in the red (idiom)
in debt (not in credit).
'If we don't get approved for the loan we'll be seriously in the red.'

in the works (idiom)
if something is in the works, it has already been planned and is ready to be worked on (also 'in the pipeline').
'We've got some exciting new projects in the works, which I'll be able to tell you more about next week.'

invoice (noun) /ˈɪnvɔɪs/
a list of all the work done and how much the work costs.
'If you could send me an invoice for all the work you've done so far, I'll send it over to the accounts department.'

invoice (verb) /ˈɪnvɔɪs/
to send a person or company a bill for the work you have done for them in order to receive payment.
'If you invoice at the end of each month for the work you've done, you'll be paid within 30 working days.'

iron (something) out (phrasal verb) /ˌaɪən ˈaʊt/
to solve any problems or sort out any details, so that something is ready for completion.
'The lawyers just need to iron out a few details in the contract and then we can sign.'

is the juice worth the squeeze? (idiom)
an informal question you ask that means 'Is all the hard work worth it for the result at the end?'
'We could rebuild the IT infrastructure, but is the juice worth the squeeze?'

it is what it is (phrase)
used to say that you must accept a situation even if you don't like it.
'I know you don't want to work over the Christmas holidays, but we need to get this campaign finished. It is what it is!'

'it is what it is'

it's not rocket science (idiom)
a phrase, often used humorously, to say that something isn't very difficult.
A – 'Are you OK to write the newsletter this week?'
B – 'Sure! It's not rocket science!'

J

jump ship (idiom)
to leave an organisation either because you have a better offer somewhere else or you think the other organisation will be more successful than your current one.
'Did you hear Dan and Tia have jumped ship and joined Open AI?'

jack of all trades (master of none) (idiom)
someone who is capable of doing many things with a reasonable level of skill but they are not an expert in one.
'I've never really specialised in anything, I'm more of a jack of all trades.'

'shall we jump on a call?'

joint venture (noun) /ˌdʒɔɪnt ˈventʃə/
a business idea that two or more people or companies work on together.
'The app is a joint venture between us and Channel 4.'

jump on a call (phrase)
to join a short phone call or meeting (also 'hop on a call').
'Shall we jump on a call later to discuss the changes?'

jump the gun (idiom)
to start doing something too early or before it should be done.
'I don't think we need to lower our prices just yet, so let's not jump the gun.'

jump through hoops (idiom)
if you jump through hoops, you do a series of boring or difficult tasks in order to achieve something.
'I had to jump through a lot of hoops to get my working visa.'

K

'we are killing it'

keep (one's) eye on the ball (idiom)
used to tell someone to pay close attention to something.
'We just need to keep our eye on the ball with this project and get it done before the deadline.'

kick (something) into the long grass (idiom)
if you kick something into the long grass, you decide to deal with it at a later point, usually because you don't want to deal with it now.
'They've decided to kick contract negotiations into the long grass.'

kick off (phrasal verb) /ˌkɪk ˈɒf/
an informal way to say 'begin'.
'I'd like to kick off this meeting by welcoming Kim to the team.'

kick the can down the road (idiom)
to delay dealing with a problem until a later date.
'It feels like we are kicking the can down the road with these necessary job cuts.'

killer (adjective) /ˈkɪlə/
successful, impressive or exciting.
'We've got a killer advertising campaign planned for this summer.'

kill it (idiom) /ˈkɪl ɪt/
an informal way to say someone is doing something extremely well.
'Have you seen the sales numbers this month? We are killing it!'

kill two birds with one stone (idiom)
to achieve two separate aims with one action.
'If we do our meeting while walking to get lunch, we can kill two birds with one stone.'

knock (something) out of the park (idiom)
to do something brilliantly (also 'hit (something) out of the park').
'Yumiko, you knocked that presentation out of the park.'

know-how (noun) /ˈnəʊˌhaʊ/
the knowledge to do something technical or practical.
'I'd love to have my own restaurant, but I don't have the know-how.'

know (something) like the back of your hand (idiom)
to be completely familiar with and knowledgeable about something.
'I think Antoni would be a great addition to the team. He knows the Eastern European market like the back of his hand.'

knuckle down (phrasal verb) /ˌnʌkəl ˈdaʊn/
to start working hard.
'Isn't it time you knuckled down and focused on your work rather than going out and having fun all the time?'

L

last minute dot com (phrase)
a very informal phrase used to say that someone does things at the last possible moment.
'Lewis is a little last minute dot com for my liking.'

lay (someone) off (phrasal verb) /ˌleɪ ˈɒf/
to stop employing someone.
'They've laid off half the staff!'

layoff (noun) /ˈleɪɒf/
the act of ending someone's employment.
'There have been widespread layoffs in the tech industry this year.'

lean in (phrasal verb) /ˌliːn ˈɪn/
to accept responsibilities and challenges that are put in front of you.
'We encourage all our grads to lean in and take on as much responsibility as they can handle.'

learning curve (noun) /ˈlɜːnɪŋ ˌkɜːv/
the rate at which someone learns a new skill.
'The learning curve on this job is very steep.'

learn the ropes (idiom)
to learn how a particular job or task is done.
'It won't take you long to learn the ropes in this job.'

leave money on the table (phrase)
to not get as much money from a deal as you could.
'It's a good deal, but I feel like they left money on the table.'

let (someone) go (phrase)
to stop someone's employment.
'The company has let three people go this week and it looks like there will be more to follow.'

level playing field (idiom)
a situation in which everyone has equal opportunities to succeed.
'The fact of the matter is, the finance industry is not a level playing field.'

leverage (noun) /ˈlevərɪdʒ/
the act of using borrowed money to buy an investment.
'They used a huge amount of leverage to buy this company and analysts are saying it's a bit of a risk.'

'learn the ropes'

leverage (noun) /ˈlevərɪdʒ/
the power to influence and get what you want.
'Let's use our leverage to ask for some more time with this deal.'

leverage (verb) /ˈlevərɪdʒ/
to use something to its maximum advantage.
'Our journalists should be leveraging the connections we have across the globe.'

liaise (with someone) (verb) /liˈeɪz/
to cooperate with people in order to share information or do a task.
'I've asked Natalia to liaise with Min-ji on the Samsung social media campaign.'

line manager (noun) /ˈlaɪn ˌmænɪdʒə/
someone who is responsible for managing staff members directly underneath them.
'If you have any questions, speak to your line manager and I'm sure they'll help you.'

line (something) up (phrasal verb) /ˌlaɪn ˈʌp/
to organise something, such as a meeting or an interview.
'I've lined up a few job interviews for next week.'

liquidation (noun) /ˌlɪkwɪˈdeɪʃən/
the process of closing a company and distributing its assets to creditors and shareholders.
'Unfortunately, after months of suffering severe losses, the company has finally gone into liquidation.'

liquidity (noun) /lɪˈkwɪdɪti/
availability of liquid assets, e.g. cash.
'The company simply doesn't have the liquidity to make it through this economic crisis.'

'People here in the UK have a love-hate relationship with business jargon like "loop (someone) in". Jargon is specialised vocabulary used by a profession or group that might be hard for outsiders to understand, and Business English is filled with it. These phrases can be a bit clichéd and cringy, but at the same time they are so commonly used and helpful, it's hard not to include them in your English.'

Teacher Tom

'lowball offer'

long shot (idiom) /ˈlɒŋ ˌʃɒt/
an attempt at something that's very unlikely to succeed, but promises great reward.
'I've applied for a job at Apple. It's a long shot, but you never know unless you try.'

look into (something) (phrasal verb) /ˌlʊk ˈɪntuː/
to investigate the facts about something.
'We've had several complaints about our servers going down. Can someone look into it for me?'

loop (someone) in (phrasal verb) /ˌluːp ˈɪn/
to include someone in a closed group so they can be kept informed about something.
'Is there anyone else you want me to loop in to this email chain?'

lowball (someone) (verb) /ˈləʊˌbɔːl/
to offer a very low amount. It can be seen as insulting to the seller.
'If they think they can lowball us like that, they've got another think coming!'

lowball offer (noun) /ˌləʊbɔːl ˈɒfə/
an offer that is much less than the seller is asking for.
'We received a lowball offer from them, but the board rejected it instantly.'

low-hanging fruit (idiom)
the obvious or easy thing that can be done or achieved.
'In order to drive profits, we need to focus on the low-hanging fruit like advertising and sponsorship.'

lucrative (adjective) /ˈluːkrətɪv/
used to describe something that makes a lot of money.
'She turned down a lucrative career in the City to work for an NGO helping refugees.'

M

make a killing (idiom)
to make a lot of money in a relatively short space of time.
'My friend Lucy has made a killing selling houses in Dubai.'

manage expectations (phrase)
to establish a realistic outcome for something in the future to avoid disappointment.
'It's important to manage your clients expectations. Don't over promise and under deliver.'

market research (noun)
/ˌmɑːkɪt ˈriːsɜːtʃ/
the act of gathering information from consumers about their needs and opinions.
'The market research shows most people prefer our new design over our old one.'

maternity leave (noun) /məˈtɜːnəti ˌliːv/
the period of time an expectant or new mother is legally entitled to have away from work (also shortened to 'mat leave').
'I'm going on mat leave in March.'

meet a deadline (phrase)
to complete a task before or by the time it must be done.
'Do you think you'll be able to meet the deadline they've set for this proposal?'

merger (noun) /ˈmɜːdʒə/
when two or more organisations join to become one bigger organisation.
'She's a consultant who specialises in mergers and acquisitions.'

micromanage (verb) /ˈmaɪkrəʊˌmænɪdʒ/
to control every detail of a project or task, even the smallest ones. It has negative connotations.
'My boss needs to give me some freedom and stop micromanaging me.'

minutes (noun) /ˈmɪnɪts/
the written record of everything that is discussed in a meeting.
'Roberto, could you do the minutes for this meeting, please?'

miss a deadline (phrase)
to fail to complete a task before it must be done.
'Make sure you get your job application in by tonight; you don't want to miss the deadline.'

mission statement (noun)
/ˈmɪʃən ˌsteɪtmənt/
a short, formal description of the aims of a company.
'In our mission statement, we clearly set out our plan to democratise the way international payments are made.'

miss the mark (idiom)
to fail to achieve the result you were aiming for.
'The CEO's speech was supposed to be reassuring, but it really missed the mark.'

monetise (verb) /ˈmʌnɪˌtaɪz/
to make money from something.
'Have you thought about monetising your Instagram account through paid sponsorship?'

‘more bang for your buck’

more bang for (one’s) buck (idiom)
better value for the money you’ve invested.
‘If we use this video-conferencing software we get more bang for our buck.’

movers and shakers (noun)
/ˌmuːvəz ən ˈʃeɪkəz/
the most influential and powerful people.
‘You should come tonight. All the movers and shakers in the industry will be there.’

move the goalposts (idiom)
to unfairly change the rules, conditions or parameters by which something should be done.
‘We thought we’d found an agreement and then at the last minute they moved the goalposts and demanded more money.’

move the needle (idiom)
to make a change that is significant and meaningful (also ‘move the dial’).
‘We’ve increased our ad spend by 20%, but that doesn’t seem to have moved the needle.’

moving parts (noun) /ˌmuːvɪŋ ˈpɑːts/
if a business has lots of moving parts, it has many interconnected components that are constantly changing and shifting.
‘I don’t think anyone realised how many moving parts there were going to be with this takeover – it’s proving more complicated than we’d anticipated.’

multinational corporation (noun)
/mʌltiˌnæʃənəl kɔːpəˈreɪʃən/
a large company that operates in multiple countries (also ‘multinational’).
‘There are calls for some of these big multinational corporations to pay more tax.’

mute (oneself) (verb) /mjuːt/
to turn the microphone on your device off so that your voice cannot be heard, e.g. on a video call.
‘Alex, we can’t hear you. I think you’ve muted yourself.’

N

network (verb) /ˈnetˌwɜːk/
to meet and interact with people who might be beneficial for your career.
'When you first start your career, take every opportunity you can to network.'

networking (noun) /ˈnetˌwɜːkɪŋ/
the act of meeting and interacting with people who might be beneficial for your career.
'KPMG have organised a networking event for all the grads tonight.'

night shift (noun) /ˈnaɪt ʃɪft/
a period of time that someone has to work in the night. It's common for security guards, doctors, nurses, hotel receptionists, etc. (also 'work nights').
'I'm not a morning person so night shifts really suit me.'

nine-to-five (adjective)
/ˌnaɪntəˈfaɪv/
describes a typical work pattern for many employees in the UK; work starts at 9 a.m. and finishes at 5 p.m. and runs from Monday to Friday.
'I just need a regular nine-to-five job to pay the bills while I write my book.'

no-brainer (noun) /ˌnəʊˈbreɪnə/
a decision that requires no thought because the answer is clear.
'Our first restaurant was so successful it meant opening our second was an absolute no- brainer.'

not have a leg to stand on (idiom)
to have no facts or evidence to support your case.
'I wouldn't worry – legally they don't have a leg to stand on.'

not know the first thing about (something) (phrase)
used to emphasise that someone doesn't know anything about a particular subject.
'My boss doesn't know the first thing about digital marketing.'

'number-crunching'

not see the wood for the trees (idiom)
if you don't see the wood for the trees, you are so involved in the details of something that you are unable to understand the wider situation.
'Diego is so focused on the tiniest details of this project, he can't see the wood for the trees.'

no-win situation (noun)
/ˌnəʊˈwɪn sɪtʃuˌeɪʃən/
a situation in which there is no positive outcome for anyone.
'These proposed store closures just feel like a no-win situation for all concerned.'

null and void (adjective) /ˌnʌl ənd ˈvɔɪd/
if an agreement or result is null and void, it is not legally valid.
'The agreement was declared null and void after accusations of forged signatures.'

number-crunching (noun)
/ˈnʌmbəˌkrʌntʃɪŋ/
the act of doing multiple numerical calculations.
'I've done some number crunching and it looks like we've made a fifty thousand pound profit this year.'

O

off base (adjective) /ˌɒf ˈbeɪs/
if you are off base about something, you are wrong.
'I may be a little off base here, but have you noticed some friction between Sam and Kenny.'

offshoring (noun) /ˌɒfˈʃɔːrɪŋ/
relocating part of a business abroad to take advantage of cheaper costs.
'They are thinking of offshoring all their manufacturing to Mexico.'

off the shelf (phrase)
if a product is off the shelf, it is available immediately and not custom made.
'We can just use an off-the-shelf web design tool rather than getting one made bespoke.'

off the top of (one's) head (idiom)
if you say something off the top of your head, you say it quickly and using the knowledge you already have.
A – 'How many stores have they opened up in India?'
B – 'Off the top of my head, I think it's somewhere around 80 or 90.'

OK (something) (verb) /ˌəʊˈkeɪ/
if you OK something, you agree with it and allow it to happen, e.g. you might OK a plan.
'Has your manager OK'd your annual leave request?'

on a shoestring (idiom)
if you do something on a shoestring, you do it with very little money.
'This whole marketing campaign has been done on a shoestring.'

on board (idiom)
agreeing with and supportive of a plan of action.
'Sounds like everyone is on board with the new designs.'

onboard (someone) (verb) /ɒnˈbɔːd/
to make sure a new employee becomes familiar with the skills and knowledge needed to be an effective member of the organisation.
'I'm helping to onboard the new grads all this week, so I might not be around that much.'

on (someone's) end (phrase)
an informal phrase used to mean 'where you are'.
'How's everything going on your end?'

one-pager (noun) /ˌwʌnˈpeɪdʒə/
a single page that summarises a topic, e.g. a business plan, idea or project.
'Can you draft me a one-pager on your business idea and we can take it from there?'

'everyone is on board'

'London has two major financial centres: the City of London, known as the Square Mile, and Canary Wharf. All the big banks and financial institutions are located in these two places. London's media is mostly based in the West End and its tech scene can be found around Old Street in an area known as the "Silicon Roundabout".'

Teacher Tom

one-size-fits-all (adjective)
/ˌwʌnsaɪzfɪtsˈɔːl/
if you describe something as one-size-fits-all, it is suitable for a wide range of people or situations.
'They've brought in a one-size-fits-all policy on bonuses and the staff are not happy about it.'

one step forward, two steps back (idiom)
used to describe a situation in which any progress that is made is counteracted with much greater problems or difficulties. This results in the feeling that you are actually further away from your goal than before.
'I thought we'd made real progress with equality in the workplace, but after this latest incident I feel like it's one step forward, two steps back.'

ongoing (adjective) /ˌɒnˈɡəʊɪŋ/
still in progress.
'Talks with a private equity firm are ongoing, but we are fairly optimistic a deal can be struck.'

'talks are ongoing'

on hold (phrase)
if something is on hold, it is no longer happening now, but may happen in the future.
'My promotion is on hold while they finalise the new management structure.'

on the back burner (idiom)
if you put something on the back burner, you decide not to deal with it immediately because it is not the most urgent or important thing you need to do.
'Our email newsletter is on the back burner, while we focus our efforts on Instagram and TikTok.'

on the right track (idiom)
doing something in the correct way that will eventually lead to the outcome you desire (also 'on track').
'The design team is definitely on the right track with the new branding.'

on the same page (idiom)
in agreement or sharing the same outlook on something.
'We've had discussions with the owners and we are all on the same page about moving our head office to Berlin next year.'

on top of (something) (idiom)
in complete control of a situation.
A – 'Who's organising the staff Christmas party?'
B – 'Don't worry, Jade is on top of it.'

opportunity cost (noun)
/ɒpəˈtʃuːnəti ˌkɒst/
the earnings lost when one alternative is chosen instead of another.
'We can choose not to open on Sundays, but what are the opportunity costs involved?'

optics (noun) /ˈɒptɪks/
the way something appears to other people, e.g. stakeholders or the general public.
'You have to admit, the optics won't look good if we fire people just before the holiday season.'

out of (one's) depth (idiom)
in a situation where your skills and capabilities are not sufficient for the task.
'For the first three months of this job, I felt completely out of my depth.'

out of the loop (idiom)
uninformed about news or information that is shared between a closed group of people.
'I was away from the office for three days and I feel completely out of the loop.'

'opportunity cost'

out of the woods (idiom)
if you are out of the woods, you are no longer in danger and/or your problems have disappeared.
'The company isn't out of the woods yet, but we've seen profits improve dramatically over the last two quarters.'

outsource (something) (verb) /ˌaʊtˈsɔːs/
if a company outsources something, it pays for another company to do the work.
'We've outsourced our customer service centre to a company in the northeast of England.'

'out on a limb'

out on a limb (idiom)
expressing an opinion that is very different from other people and may be unpopular.
'I'm going to go out on a limb here and say this new government initiative to stimulate economic growth won't work.'

out over (one's) skis (idiom)
getting ahead of oneself. There is a sense that you've acted a little too hastily and maybe in an overly aggressive way, e.g. hired too many people too quickly.
'Pre-pandemic, we were a little too far out over our skis and hired like crazy. As a result, we've had to let a few people go.'

overheads (noun) /ˈəʊvəˌheds/
the continuing cost of running a business, e.g. electricity, rent.
'The overheads at our old office were far too expensive so we decided to move to this slightly smaller office down the road.'

overtime (noun) /ˈəʊvəˌtaɪm/
the work that is done beyond an employee's scheduled working hours (also 'OT').
'I've worked 20 hours of overtime this month.'

P

pain point (noun) /ˈpeɪn ˌpɔɪnt/
a specific problem faced by a potential or current customer.
'The first thing you need to do is identify your potential customers' pain points so you can start finding ways to solve them.'

paperwork (noun) /ˈpeɪpəˌwɜːk/
the aspect of work that involves writing and recording information e.g. forms or contracts.
'I didn't realise running a coffee shop would require so much paperwork.'

park (something) (verb) /pɑːk/
to leave a task incomplete for a period of time while you focus on other things.
'Let's park this conversation here and come back to it when we have more time.'

pass the buck (idiom)
to not take responsibility for something going wrong and blaming someone else.
'I can't believe he's trying to pass the buck when the entire mess-up was his fault.'

paternity leave (noun) /pəˈtɜːnɪti ˌliːv/
the period of time a new father is legally entitled to take away from work (also shortened to 'pat leave').
'When does your paternity leave begin?'

pay band (noun) /ˈpeɪ ˌbænd/
a level of salary that a business offers for a certain job or degree of responsibility.
'All the grads started on the same pay band.'

peel (back) the onion (idiom)
to thoroughly analyse or expose something, layer by layer, in order to understand it.
'We really need to peel back the onion on what went wrong last quarter so we don't make the same mistakes again.'

pencil (something) in (phrasal verb) /ˌpensəl ˈɪn/
to make a plan or arrangement knowing that the details, such as the date or time, might change.
'Let's pencil in a catch-up for tomorrow at two.'

'peel back the onion'

TOM'S TIPS

There are so many vivid and creative ways to describe the rise and fall of numbers. For example, if something goes down rapidly, we can say 'plummet', 'nose dive' or 'plunge'. If it rises, we can say 'surge', 'rocket' or 'soar'. These are great for describing the change in a company's share price or the figures in a sales report.

perk (noun) /pɜːk/
an extra benefit, e.g. money or a gift.
'One of the perks of working here is that you get free gym membership at Third Space.'

pick (someone's) brains (idiom)
to get information from someone who is more knowledgeable on a topic than you.
'Sachin, could I just pick your brains about the new tax laws for EU-based companies?'

ping (verb) /pɪŋ/
to send a message, email or other electronic communication to someone.
'Can you ping me Isabel's number so I can call her?'

pinpoint (verb) /ˈpɪnˌpɔɪnt/
to find or identify a very specific thing.
'Did you manage to pinpoint exactly what the issue was with the website this morning?'

pitch (verb) /pɪtʃ/
if you pitch an idea, suggestion or concept, you present it with the aim of getting approval or financial support.
'Kelly and I are pitching a new TV format to some BBC execs this afternoon, so we'll be out of the office.'

pitch in (phrasal verb) /ˌpɪtʃˈɪn/
to join and contribute to a group task or activity.
'Do you mind if I pitch in with a few ideas for how I think the design could look?'

pivot (verb) /ˈpɪvət/
to shift the direction of a business in order to pursue greater sales.
'I think we should pivot slightly and start targeting the domestic market.'

play hardball (idiom)
to negotiate or do business in a tough, determined way.
'Her agent is playing hardball, but I'm hopeful we can get the appearance fee down.'

play it by ear (idiom)
to make decisions about a plan or idea as things progress and become clearer.
'I don't know how many people are going to attend the workshop tomorrow, so let's play it by ear.'

play second fiddle (idiom)
to play a supporting or less important role to someone else.
'Richard and I are on the same pay band, and yet I feel like I have to play second fiddle to him all the time.'

plug-and-play (adjective) /ˌplʌɡənˈpleɪ/
ready to use immediately.
'We are looking for a plug-and-play solution for our internal communications.'

plummet (verb) /ˈplʌmɪt/
to fall very quickly and suddenly.
'Sales plummeted in Q4.'

plunge (verb) /plʌndʒ/
to fall very quickly and suddenly.
'The stock price has plunged after the earnings report was released.'

point of sale (noun) /ˌpɔɪnt əv ˈseɪl/
anywhere in which a transaction for a product or service can take place.
'What's the customer experience like at the point of sale?'

point out (phrasal verb) /ˌpɔɪnt ˈaʊt/
to bring someone's attention to something.
'It's important to point out that we are only two weeks into this project, so there are going to be some teething problems.'

polish (something) off (phrasal verb) /ˌpɒlɪʃ ˈɒf/
to finish something completely in a quick, easy fashion.
'I need to polish off this email, then I'm free to go.'

presenteeism (noun) /ˌprezənˈtiːɪzm/
the performative act of remaining longer at work than you are required to, in order to show you are a valuable, hard-working employee.
'Companies are trying to crack down on employees engaging in presenteeism, as it harms both parties in the long run.'

price point (noun) /ˈpraɪs ˌpɔɪnt/
the selling price set for a service or product.
'At this price point, I think it's going to be really hard to sell many units.'

probationary period (noun) /prəˈbeɪʃənəri ˌpɪəriəd/
a period of time at the beginning of someone's employment, used to assess if they are the right fit for the role.
'We usually include a three-month probationary period for all new hires.'

profitable (adjective) /ˈprɒfɪtəbəl/
if something is profitable, it makes more money than it costs.
'Getting our merchandise made print-on-demand is proving to be so much more profitable.'

projection (noun) /prəˈdʒekʃən/
an estimate or forecast.
'What's the projection for our fourth-quarter revenue?'

TOM'S TIPS

There's so much push and pull in the world of Business English, and many of our phrases invite you to imagine the physical act. A good example is to 'pull the strings', which means to control a situation just like a puppet master pulls the strings of a puppet to control it. Likewise, to 'push back on (something)' suggests we physically repel an idea with our arms. I love the physicality of language!

‘pushback’

pull a late one (phrase)
an informal way to say ‘work very late’.
‘You look like you pulled a late one last night!’

pull the plug (on something) (idiom)
to stop supporting a project or activity so that it cannot continue.
‘They’ve pulled the plug on all research funding, so my team won’t be heading out to Kenya this year.’

pull the strings (idiom)
to have control over a situation or person, often in secret.
‘Their former CEO stepped down last year, but I suspect he’s still pulling the strings.’

pull the trigger (on something) (idiom)
to commit to a final decision.
‘Did you see they finally pulled the trigger on the Dyson deal?’

pull (something) together (phrasal verb)
/ˌpʊl təˈgeðə/
to collect parts of something to make it complete, e.g. information, numbers and stats for a presentation.
‘Natasha and Marcel are pulling together the Coca-Cola presentation for us.’

pull (one’s) weight (idiom)
to work as hard as anyone else and do your fair share of work.
‘How are Ella and Sergio settling in to your team? Are they pulling their weight?’

pushback (noun) /ˈpʊʃˌbæk/
resistance to a new idea or plan.
‘There has been a lot of pushback from our investors.’

push (something) back (phrasal verb)
/ˌpʊʃˈbæk/
to delay something, e.g. a meeting.
‘They’ve pushed back our weekly call to tomorrow.’

push back on (something) (phrasal verb)
/ˌpʊʃˈbæk ɒn/
if you push back on something, such as a policy or a piece of work, you refuse to accept it or try to prevent it.
‘There are a few points in the contract that we’ll need to push back on.’

put a pin in (something) (idiom)
a phrase used to suggest coming back to an idea or suggestion.
‘OK team, let’s put a pin in that idea and move on to the next item on the agenda.’

put in a good word (for someone) (idiom)
to say positive things about someone, usually to help them in some way.
‘I’m applying for a new role and I wondered if you could speak to my manager and put in a good word for me.’

put out fires (idiom)
to deal with small problems.
‘I haven’t managed to sit down once today. I’ve just been putting out fires all day.’

put (something) together (phrasal verb)
/ˌpʊt təˈgeðə/
to prepare a piece of work by collecting ideas into one place.
‘Management have put together a proposal to save the company from bankruptcy.’

Q

quarter (noun) /ˈkwɔːtə/
a three-month period in an organisation's financial year, e.g. first quarter, second quarter.
'Our third-quarter profits were surprisingly healthy compared to the previous two quarters.'

quick win (noun) /ˌkwɪk ˈwɪn/
an improvement that is easy to do and has immediate benefits.
'It's important to get your client a couple of quick wins right at the beginning.'

quid pro quo (noun) /ˌkwɪd prəʊ ˈkwəʊ/
the exchange of one thing for another, often of equal value.
'Offering them a bit more money is quid pro quo for the services they'll provide.'

quit (verb) /kwɪt/
to resign from a job.
'Three board members have quit in the last month.'

'quick win'

R

raise the bar (idiom)
to set higher standards than anything that has come before.
'The technical brilliance of some of these app designers in London is raising the bar for others to follow.'

ramp (something) up (phrasal verb) /ˌræmp ˈʌp/
to increase the level or amount of something by a lot.
'We need to ramp up production if we are going to fulfil all our clothing orders.'

rattle through (something) (phrasal verb) /ˌrætəl ˈθruː/
to do or say something in a hurry.
'Let's rattle through this meeting so we can all get out of here by six.'

reach out to (someone) (phrasal verb) /ˌriːtʃ ˈaʊt tuː/
to make contact with someone in order to talk to them or offer help.
'Sam Wong from HR reached out the other day to see if we want to help out with some of the training sessions next week.'

read between the lines (idiom)
to understand the implied meaning of what someone has said or done.
'Reading between the lines, I'd say we've got a good chance of persuading them to switch their account over to us.'

red tape (idiom)
an excessive amount of unnecessary rules and administration.
'There's so much red tape trying to sell goods in the EU now, we've simply stopped trying.'

redundancy package (noun) /rɪˈdʌndənsi ˌpækɪdʒ/
the financial offer a company gives employers who have lost their job.
'The redundancy package they were offering was very generous.'

redundant (adjective) /rɪˈdʌndənt/
if you are made redundant, you lose your job.
'My flatmate has just been made redundant.'

reinvent the wheel (idiom)
to waste time trying to do something that has already been done before.
'We've got a perfectly good social media strategy, let's not try to reinvent the wheel with a new one.'

relieve (someone) of their duties/ responsibilities (phrase)
to stop employing someone. Quite formal usage.
'After a turbulent year, the board has decided to relieve the CEO of their duties.'

remote working (noun) /rɪˌməʊt ˈwɜːkɪŋ/
a flexible working arrangement in which employees are able to work in locations other than the main centralised office.
'Remote working has really changed the way people think about where they want to live.'

ring-fence (verb) /ˈrɪŋˌfens/
to put protections around an amount of money and make sure it is used for a specific purpose.
'They've ring-fenced 20 million pounds to pay for a new research and development team.'

'remote working'

rep (noun) /rep/
a person who works in an official capacity for a company, e.g. a holiday rep or a sales rep (short for 'representative').
'I was a holiday rep in Greece during my summer holidays at uni.'

resign (verb) /rɪˈzaɪn/
to leave your job by choice.
'The reason I resigned is because I didn't feel supported by management.'

restructuring (noun) /ˌriːˈstrʌktʃərɪŋ/
the process of changing the way a business is organised and operates in order to make it more efficient and successful.
'There's going to be a lot of restructuring in the new year and I'm a little worried about my job.'

right-size (verb) /ˈraɪtˌsaɪz/
to improve the performance of a company that has been struggling, usually by making it smaller.
'They've brought in a top consultancy firm to right-size the business.'

roadmap (noun) /ˈrəʊdˌmæp/
a plan for how to achieve a specific business goal.
'Let's sketch out a roadmap to profitability.'

rock the boat (idiom)
to say or do something that destabilises a calm situation.
'I'm new to the company and I don't want to rock the boat, but I've not been very impressed with Andrew's management style so far.'

roll off (phrasal verb) /ˌrəʊl ˈɒf/
to finish working on a project or within a programme.
'We are due to roll off the Bloomberg project next month.'

roll (something) out (phrasal verb) /ˌrəʊl ˈaʊt/
to officially launch a new product or service.
'Apple is rolling out the new iPhone early next year.'

roll up (one's) sleeves (idiom)
to get ready to work hard.
'It's time to roll up our sleeves and get this presentation finished.'

TOM'S TIPS

Another great trick proficient English speakers use to sound more fluent is to use linking to blend words together, especially phrasal verbs. This happens when one word ends in a consonant sound and the next word begins with a vowel sound. For example 'roll off' /rəʊ lɒf/ and 'roll out' /rəʊ laʊt/. Can you find more examples?

rubber-stamp (verb) /ˌrʌbəˈstæmp/
to give official approval to something without full and proper consideration.
'They've rubber-stamped the decision to switch our operations to Singapore without any consultation.'

rule of thumb (idiom)
a general simplified rule that guides people's actions.
'As a general rule of thumb, we tend to have our lunches at our desks.'

rule (something) out (phrasal verb) /ˌruːl ˈaʊt/
to exclude something or someone as a possibility.
'We can't rule out the possibility of a recession early next year.'

run a tight ship (idiom)
to run something in a very controlled, disciplined way.
'Shana runs a very tight ship. Her team always delivers results.'

run (something) by (someone) (phrasal verb) /ˌrʌn ˈbaɪ/
to explain or tell someone an idea in order to get their opinion or approval (also 'run something past somebody').
'Let's run that by HR and see what they say.'

run (something) into the ground (idiom)
to manage a company so badly that it's in danger of going out of business.
'Since the takeover, the new owners have run this business into the ground.'

run the numbers (phrase)
to do the calculations.
'Before we make any decisions, let's run the numbers and see how much of the budget we still have available.'

run (something) up the flagpole (idiom)
to float an idea to see what the reaction is.
'That's an interesting idea. Why don't you run it up the flagpole at the next meeting.'

runway (noun) /ˈrʌnˌweɪ/
the amount of time a new business can operate before it runs out of money.
'We've got a six-month runway before we are in real trouble.'

run with (something) (phrasal verb) /ˈrʌn ˌwɪð/
to take an idea or method and develop it, often enthusiastically.
'We showed the Malaysian team how to use our new system and they've just run with it.'

S

sack (verb) /sæk/
to end someone's employment.
'They sacked him via email after 30 years of service to the company.'

safe bet (idiom)
something that is extremely likely to be true or happen.
'There's no such thing as a safe bet in the stock market.'

sales funnel (noun) /ˈseɪlz ˌfʌnəl/
the entire sales journey a customer goes through from awareness to purchase.
'Our revenue has grown significantly since improving our sales funnel.'

scalable (adjective) /ˈskeɪləbəl/
if something is scalable, it can grow to meet increased demand.
'This business model is completely scalable because you can sell it to one person or one million people and it's the same amount of work.'

scale (something) back (phrasal verb) /ˌskeɪl ˈbæk/
to make something smaller in size or scope.
'They've had to scale back their operations in Ireland as it was proving far too costly.'

scale (something) up (phrasal verb) /ˌskeɪl ˈʌp/
to grow or expand something, e.g. an organisation.
'We are starting to scale up our presence in Asia.'

see eye to eye (idiom)
to agree.
'It's not the first time my boss and I haven't seen eye to eye on things.'

see (something) through (phrasal verb) /ˌsiː ˈθruː/
to continue to do something until the end, often something that is not easy.
'I'm determined to see this project through, and then I'm booking myself a very long and well-deserved holiday.'

sell like hot cakes (idiom)
used to describe a product or service that is very popular and sells quickly.
'The new Givenchy perfume is selling like hot cakes.'

sever ties with (someone) (idiom)
to end an agreement or relationship with someone.
'We've decided to sever ties with the charity after allegations of bullying and harassment.'

TOM'S TIPS

In English, we say something 'sells like hot cakes', whereas in German, things 'sell like sliced bread' and in Spanish they 'sell like churros'. Is there a similar expression in your language?

‘a quick show of hands’

shareholder (noun) /ˈʃeəˌhəʊldə/
someone who owns shares in a company.
‘There’s a shareholders’ meeting next month that will decide who the next chairperson is going to be.’

shelve (verb) /ʃelv/
if you shelve a plan or project, you decide not to proceed with it until a later date.
‘The government has shelved plans to abolish the top tax rate.’

shift (noun) /ʃɪft/
a period of time that someone has to work that’s outside the ‘normal’ nine to five, e.g. 6 a.m. to 2 p.m. It’s usually used in the retail and service industries as well as the emergency services.
‘I’m doing the morning shift today so I’ll be home around 3 p.m.’

shirk (verb) /ʃɜːk/
to avoid or neglect to do something, e.g. work or a responsibility or duty.
‘I don’t want to shirk my responsibility, but don’t you think it should be senior management’s job to fire people, not ours?’

shoot (oneself) in the foot (idiom)
to make a situation worse for yourself, by accident.
‘I’ve really shot myself in the foot with my boss! I accidentally sent them an email questioning their leadership skills that was meant for someone else.’

short-staffed (adjective) /ˌʃɔːtˈstɑːft/
not having enough staff to do the necessary tasks.
‘We are a little short-staffed today, so I’ve asked Justine to come in on her day off.’

show of hands (noun) /ʃəʊ əv ˈhændz/
an informal vote in which the people involved raise their hand in the air to indicate their support.
‘Can we have a quick show of hands to see who still wants to go ahead with the event?’

sick leave (noun) /ˈsɪk ˌliːv/
time spent away from work because of illness or injury.
‘Esteban is on sick leave today, so I’d like you to make his sales calls for him.’

side hustle (noun) /ˈsaɪd ˌhʌsəl/
the work you do and get paid for, in addition to your main job.
‘I started this company originally as a side hustle, before going full-time three years ago.’

sign off on (something) (phrasal verb) /ˌsaɪn ˈɒf ɒn/
to give something official approval.
‘I just need to get HR to sign off on it and then you are free to book your holiday.’

sing from the same hymn sheet (idiom)
used to say that a group of people are all in agreement with each other and expressing the same opinion in public, even though they might not all agree privately.
'After long negotiations, it feels like we've got everyone singing from the same hymn sheet.'

sit in on (something) (phrasal verb) /ˌsɪt ˈɪn ɒn/
to attend a meeting or class, but with the intention of observing not participating.
'Would you mind if I sit in on your client meeting, so I can learn the ropes?'

skill set (noun) /ˈskɪl ˌset/
the various things someone is good at, relating to their ability to do a job.
'You need a very specific skill set to be able to survive in this cut-throat environment.'

slack off (phrasal verb) /ˌslæk ˈɒf/
to put less effort into your work.
'You'll notice people in the office tend to slack off a little bit on Friday afternoons.'

slide deck (noun) /ˈslaɪd ˌdek/
a collection of slides used as a visual aid in a presentation.
'We've prepared a slide deck for the Uber meeting, if you'd like to see it before we go in.'

small talk (noun) /ˈsmɔːl ˌtɔːk/
conversation about very general everyday topics, e.g. the weather.
'If there's one thing I hate about meetings, it's the small talk at the beginning.'

smooth sailing (idiom)
if something is smooth sailing, it's easy to make progress without any problems (also 'plain sailing').
'Ever since we brought in a team coordinator, it's been smooth sailing.'

snowed under (idiom)
having too much work to do.
'I'm afraid I can't come out tonight. I'm snowed under with work right now.'

soft skills (noun) /ˈsɒft ˌskɪlz/
the interpersonal skills to communicate and work with other people.
'An important part of our grad scheme is dedicated to helping newcomers improve their soft skills.'

sounds about right (phrase)
an informal phrase used to agree with someone, even though you can't be 100 per cent sure.
A – 'Shall we keep the guest list for the event to less than a hundred?'
B – 'Yeah that sounds about right.'

'that sounds about right'

spike (noun) /spaɪk/
a very quick rise in the price, volume or amount of something, usually before a fall.
'There was a spike in mortgage approvals in December and January.'

spike (verb) /spaɪk/
if something spikes, it rises very quickly, usually before a fall.
'Unemployment rates have spiked after the news of supply-chain issues.'

'stay in your lane'

spin (something) off (phrasal verb)
/ˌspɪn ˈɒf/
to separate a piece of a company so that it becomes an independent business.
'There are rumours that we'll try to spin off our media division at some point next year.'

square the circle (idiom)
to attempt to solve a problem or do something that's very difficult or almost impossible.
'They are trying to square the circle by bringing in more regulation and also driving profits.'

stakeholder (noun) /ˈsteɪkˌhəʊldə/
an individual or group that has a close interest in the outcome of a project or business.
'We've got several meetings with stakeholders booked in for next week.'

standing meeting (noun)
/ˌstændɪŋ ˈmiːtɪŋ/
a meeting that is scheduled to repeat on a regular basis at the same time (also 'stand-up meeting').
'Let's set up a standing meeting for Mondays at 9 a.m.'

startup (noun) /ˈstɑːtˌʌp/
a new business.
'Safiya left the US to join a tech startup in Hyderabad.'

start (something) up (phrasal verb)
/ˌstɑːt ˈʌp/
to create and begin to operate a new company.
'I've heard you are starting up your own online clothing company, is that right?'

stay in (one's) lane (idiom)
used to tell someone to stick to what they know or what they are good at.
'I'd advise you to stay in your lane and not give the marketing team unsolicited advice.'

steering committee (noun)
/ˈstɪərɪŋ kəˌmɪti/
a group of high-level people who advise on the direction a business should go.
'We've assembled a very experienced steering committee to help see us through this first year in business.'

step down (phrasal verb) /ˌstep ˈdaʊn/
to resign from a job, role or position.
'Fergal is stepping down as CTO with immediate effect.'

stopgap measure (noun)
/ˈstɒpgæp ˌmeʒə/
a temporary solution that will work until a permanent solution is found.
'This video-conferencing tool is fine as a stopgap measure, but we need to find a more reliable solution quickly.'

strategise (verb) /ˈstrætəˌdʒaɪz/
to think of a plan or course of action.
'Get everyone on a call and let's strategise a possible response to these media reports.'

'stopgap measure'

step on (someone's) toes (idiom)
to offend or upset someone by doing something that is designated as their responsibility (also 'tread on (someone's) toes').
'Will I be stepping on anyone's toes if I take charge of organising the staff summer party?'

step up (one's) game (idiom)
to try harder and improve your skills or performance.
'I realise I need to step up my game if I'm going to get a promotion this year.'

step up to the plate (idiom)
to accept the challenge and responsibility of something, at a time when it is needed.
'You've really stepped up to the plate while Valentina has been on sick leave.'

sterling (noun) /ˈstɜːlɪŋ/
the currency in Great Britain.
'Do you know where I can change these Euros into sterling?'

streamline (verb) /ˈstriːmˌlaɪn/
to improve the efficiency of a company, department or process by simplifying or removing unnecessary work.
'We're looking to streamline all of our overseas operations.'

stumbling block (noun) /ˈstʌmbəlɪŋ ˌblɒk/
a problem that gets in the way of progress or an agreement.
'We've hit a couple of stumbling blocks with the British Airways deal.'

supply chain (noun) /səˈplaɪ ˌtʃeɪn/
the network of people, organisations, materials and technology that help take a product from its creation to the customer.
'The accident in the Suez Canal affected the global supply chain in a really negative way.'

swamped (adjective) /swɒmpt/
having a huge amount of work to do.
'I'm absolutely swamped at work, so I don't think I'll be home for dinner.'

T

table (something) (verb) /ˈteɪbəl/
to raise a topic for formal discussion.
'I'm going to table my new vision for the company at the team meeting today.'

tailwind (noun) /ˈteɪlˌwɪnd/
a positive factor that could lead to higher profits or growth.
'Certainly the proposed tax cuts will act as a bit of a tailwind for us.'

take a back seat (idiom)
to choose to be less involved or active with something.
'Maria has chosen to take a back seat on this campaign, so that you and I can run it the way we want.'

take a stab at (something) (idiom)
to try to do something, knowing that you might not be successful (also 'have/make a stab at something).
'I've never done one of these before, but I'm willing to take a stab at it.'

takeaway (noun) /ˈteɪkəˌweɪ/
the main point or learning point.
'What are the key takeaways from this meeting?'

take (someone) down a peg or two (idiom)
to make someone feel they are less important than they think they are.
'I know I shouldn't think this, but it was nice to see my horrible manager taken down a peg or two by the CEO.'

take (something) offline (phrase)
to talk about something away from the current situation, e.g. a meeting.
'If you'd like to know more details about the case, I'm happy to take it offline with you after the meeting.'

take (something) on board (phrase)
to understand and consider an issue or matter.
'We've taken our customers' feedback on board and started to make big changes to the way we communicate as a company.'

TOM'S TIPS

As if learning English wasn't hard enough, it turns out there are some words that can be used in completely different ways depending on where you are in the world. One particular example is the verb 'to table (something)'. In the UK, we use it to bring forward an idea for discussion, whereas in the USA it means to delay or postpone talking about it. The complete opposite!

'teething problems'

take one for the team (idiom)
to sacrifice yourself for the greater good of the team. This might mean doing extra work or accepting blame for a mistake, etc.
'Can we all show a little love for Kyle? He took one for the team and spent his entire weekend translating our business presentation into Spanish!'

take the bull by the horns (idiom)
to take control and deal with a difficult situation in a confident, direct way.
'If you want to make any sales, you've got to take the bull by the horns and start making calls.'

take the lead on (something) (phrase)
to accept responsibility for something collaborative, e.g. a project.
'Yen is going to take the lead on the Starbucks campaign, so if you have any questions send them her way.'

take (someone) under your wing (idiom)
to protect someone, give them guidance and make sure they are OK.
'It's nice to see you've taken the new intern under your wing.'

talk (someone) into (something)
(phrasal verb) /ˌtɔːk ˈɪntuː/
to convince someone to do something.
'Has Fernando managed to talk you into coming out after work?'

talk (someone) out of (something)
(phrasal verb) /ˌtɔːk ˈaʊt əv/
to convince someone not to do something.
'No, I've actually talked Fernando out of going! We're doing hot yoga instead.'

talk shop (idiom)
to talk about work with people you work with, while not at work.
'Can you stop talking shop! This is supposed to be a party.'

task (someone) with (something)
(phrasal verb) /tɑːsk/
to assign a task to someone. It's often used in the passive.
'I've been tasked with writing the newsletter this week.'

team building (noun) /ˈtiːm ˌbɪldɪŋ/
activities designed to help form strong connections among a group of colleagues. This is often done through facilitated challenges.
'We've got a team-building event next Friday where we'll do a treasure hunt around London.'

team huddle (noun) /ˌtiːm ˈhʌdəl/
a quick, informal type of meeting usually used to brief the team on that day's news or agenda.
'Let's have a team huddle at 10 a.m. and we can go through what needs to be done today.'

teething problems (idiom)
minor problems at the beginning of a business, project or product launch.
'The website is experiencing a few teething problems, but we've got a really good team working on it.'

temp (noun) /temp/
a temporary member of staff.
'They've hired a temp to run the customer service desk while Stefan is on holiday.'

temping (noun) /ˈtempɪŋ/
temporary work.
'I did a lot of temping while I was studying at university.'

the $64,000 question (phrase)
the most important question that is difficult to answer (also 'million dollar question').
'The $64,000 question is, are we heading into a recession later this year?'

the ball is in (someone's) court (idiom)
used to tell someone that it is their turn to take action if any progress is to be made.
'We've made our position clear, so now the ball is very much in their court. Let's see what they decide to do.'

the bare minimum (phrase)
the very least you can do.
'He comes into work and just does the bare minimum! Someone's got to have a word with him.'

the big/bigger picture (idiom)
the situation as a whole.
'I know the results haven't been great, but if you look at the bigger picture they aren't actually that bad.'

the bottom line (noun) /ˌbɒtəm ˈlaɪn/
the final line on a company's accounts stating if it has made a profit or loss.
'This economic downturn is going to impact our bottom line in a severe way.'

the buck stops here (idiom)
said by someone who is taking responsibility for the decisions they make and any criticism they might get as a result (also 'the buck stops with (someone)').
'I don't want to hear any more excuses! Ultimately the buck stops here, with us, so let's get the problem fixed as soon as possible.'

the final straw (idiom)
the last incident in a series of difficult or unpleasant events that makes someone think they cannot continue to accept a bad situation.
'I've been unhappy with my boss for a while, but this latest confrontation is the final straw. I'm going to lodge a formal complaint.'

'the final straw'

the home stretch (idiom)
the final part of a long or difficult activity (also 'the home straight').
'Putting this publication together has been a real challenge, but we are on the home stretch.'

the long haul (idiom)
a long period of time.
'The company's investment strategy has been successful over the long haul.'

the proof is in the pudding (idiom)
a phrase used to say that we can only judge the success of something once we have tried or tested it (also 'the proof is in the eating').
'I think you'll love Virgin's new business class lounge at Heathrow, but the proof is in the pudding.'

TOM'S TIPS

Shapes play a key role in Business English idioms. We think outside boxes, we square circles, we cut corners and we are ahead of curves. Look for other examples in this A–Z section.

the tail wagging the dog (idiom)
a situation in which the smaller part of something controls the larger part and has influence over it.
'For years, lower league football teams in England dictated terms for TV deals. Then in 1992, the elite teams established the Premier League. It was a classic case of the tail wagging the dog.'

the top line (noun) /ˌtɒp ˈlaɪn/
the first line on a company's accounts that states the total gross revenue.
'There are a few strategies we could employ to help grow our top line.'

the writing is on the wall (idiom)
a phrase used to say that there are obvious indicators something is going to end badly or go wrong.
'I'm not surprised they are struggling financially. The writing has been on the wall for a long time.'

think on (one's) feet (phrase)
to think of ideas or make decisions quickly without time to prepare.
'They fired some really tough questions at me in the interview, so I had to think on my feet quite a few times.'

think outside the box (idiom)
to think in new, creative and unconventional ways that are different to how you've thought before.
'I want you all to think outside the box on this one. Let's really push our creativity with this campaign.'

thread the needle (idiom)
to skilfully handle and navigate a difficult problem.
'When it comes to these very delicate situations around work and social justice issues, the leadership team is really good at threading the needle.'

throw (someone) in at the deep end (idiom)
if you are thrown in at the deep end, you are put in a completely new situation that you have no experience of dealing with.
'We like to throw our grads in at the deep end on day one and get them pitching to potential clients.'

throw in the towel (idiom)
to give up trying to do something because you realise you won't succeed.
'The other firm has thrown in the towel, which leaves us as the only bidder left.'

throw (someone) under the bus (idiom)
to cause someone else to get the blame for something, in order to avoid it yourself.
'I can't believe he threw you under the bus like that when it's his mistake in the first place.'

tick-box exercise (noun)
/ˈtɪkbɒks ˌeksəsaɪz/
a task or process that is only done to satisfy rules or normal conventions (see also 'box ticking').
'This team review just feels like a tick-box exercise.'

tighten (one's) belt (idiom)
to spend less money than you previously did.
'We're going to have to tighten our belts for a while; no more expensive corporate lunches.'

time off in lieu (noun) /ˌtaɪm ɒf ɪn ˈljuː/
time off because you have worked extra hours (also known as 'TOIL').
'I worked over the weekend, so I've got some time off in lieu.'

time-sensitive (adjective) /ˈtaɪmˌsensɪtɪv/
if something is time-sensitive, it needs to be completed or used by a specific time.
'Could you get back to me on this, it's time-sensitive.'

toe the line (idiom)
to follow the rules and expectations placed upon you by an authority.
'I find it hard to toe the company line when they are doing so many terrible things to the environment.'

too many cooks spoil the broth (idiom)
used to say that if too many people are involved in an activity it won't be done well. With well-known phrases like this, it's sometimes OK just to say the first part, i.e. 'too many cooks'.
'Cherry, you take the lead on this and the rest of us can take a step back. Too many cooks and all that.'

top-down (adjective) /ˌtɒpˈdaʊn/
involving a system in which decisions are made at the highest level.
'This top-down approach to decision-making has left the people on the office floor a little disgruntled.'

touch base (idiom)
to make contact with someone.
'Let's touch base tomorrow and decide what to do then.'

touchpoint (noun) /ˈtʌtʃˌpɔɪnt/
any direct or indirect contact a business has with its customers.
'The sheer number of digital touchpoints we have with our customers has meant we know their wants and needs so much better than before.'

town hall (noun) /ˌtaʊn ˈhɔːl/
an official meeting where a business leader or politician presents their policies and answers questions from the attendees.
'The CEO has arranged a town hall to explain her vision for the company going forward.'

traction (noun) /ˈtrækʃən/
if something gains traction, it starts to be successful and popular.
'Our monthly webinars are really gaining traction.'

tread water (idiom)
to fail to make any progress.
'After five years in this job, I feel like I'm treading water. It's time for a new challenge.'

'let's touch base'

troubleshoot (verb) /ˈtrʌbəlˌʃuːt/
to try and diagnose why something isn't working, e.g. a computer program.
'Can we get one of the IT team in to troubleshoot this "system error" message we keep getting?'

turnaround (noun) /ˈtɜːnəˌraʊnd/
the amount of time it takes for a task or piece of work to be done.
'We've got a bit of a tight turnaround on this proposal, so I'll probably be working late tonight.'

turn (something) down (phrasal verb) /ˌtɜːn ˈdaʊn/
to reject an offer or invitation.
'I've decided to turn down the job offer from Unilever.'

turnover (noun) /ˈtɜːnˌəʊvə/
the total sales made by a business in a certain amount of time.
'Our turnover has doubled in the last 18 months.'

tweak (something) (verb) /twiːk/
to adjust something by a little bit in order to make it better.
'I've tweaked the presentation so the font is a little easier to read.'

twist (someone's) arm (idiom)
to convince someone to do something they don't necessarily want to do.
'Alright, you've twisted my arm! I'll come to the social for an hour, but then I'm going home.'

'The UK economy is dominated by services, with hospitality, retail, technology and finance leading the way. The UK also has a thriving creative industry producing films, TV shows, music and fashion that are known all over the world. Healthcare plays a huge part in the UK economy; big global pharmaceutical companies are headquartered here and the NHS is the nation's largest employer. While smaller industries such as agriculture and manufacturing have reduced in size over the years, they remain vitally important in this globalised world.'

Teacher Tom

U

unpack (something) (verb) /ʌnˈpæk/
to examine or analyse something to try to understand it better.
'Have you had a chance to unpack what the CFO said in their speech?'

up against it (idiom)
facing a difficult situation or set of circumstances.
'We've got quite a few staff members off sick this week so we're going to be up against it.'

up in the air (idiom)
if something is up in the air, it is undecided or uncertain.
'If we can't secure financing quickly, this whole project will be up in the air.'

uphill battle (noun)
if something is described as an uphill battle, it can be challenging, difficult and a struggle to complete.
'It's going to be a real uphill battle to turn this company around, but I love a challenge.'

upside (noun) /ˈʌpˌsaɪd/
the benefit or positive aspect of something.
'Switching providers is going to cost us an extra £1,000 a month so what's the upside on this?'

upskill (verb) /ˌʌpˈskɪl/
to provide employees with more advanced training and skills.
'It's vitally important we upskill our workforce if we are going to compete in this market.'

up to (one's) neck in (something) (idiom)
having more work than you can handle (also 'up to (one's) eyeballs in (something)').
'I've been up to my neck in paperwork all day.'

up to speed (idiom)
if you are up to speed, you are fully informed about something.
'Yasmin, can you bring everyone up to speed with the latest on the Sony deal?'

user experience (noun)
/ˈjuːzə ɪkˌspɪəriəns/
the overall experience someone has of using a product, i.e. do they find it easy, difficult, enjoyable, etc.
'We have to focus on creating a phenomenal user experience for our new smartphones.'

'U-turn'

U-turn (noun) /ˈjuːˌtɜːn/
a decision or plan that is completely reversed because the original idea was wrong.
'The government has been forced to make a big U-turn on their plan to raise corporation tax.

V

value-add (noun) /ˈvælju:ˌæd/
something that provides extra benefit.
'The new voice-activated feature is a real value-add.'

variable costs (noun) /ˈveəriəbəl ˌkɒsts/
costs that change depending on the amount of business a company does, e.g. bonuses, shipping or supplies.
'Our variable costs sky-rocketed during the supply-chain issues.'

vertical integration (noun) /ˌvɜ:tɪkəl ɪntɪˈgreɪʃən/
a strategy in which a business owns all aspects of production, i.e. the complete supply chain. The reason for this is so that it doesn't have to rely on any external companies for the creation of its goods or services.
'Vertical integration for Tesla was an absolute game-changer.'

vertical market (noun) /ˌvɜ:tɪkəl ˈmɑ:kɪt/
a specific industry or market that focuses on servicing a particular niche (also 'vertical').
'The plant-based-food vertical is growing rapidly as demand from consumers increases.'

vested interest (noun) /ˌvestɪd ˈɪntrɪst/
a personal reason for wanting something to happen, often because of a financial or direct gain.
'As both an employee and a shareholder, I have a vested interest in seeing this business thrive.'

'vis-à-vis'

vis-à-vis (preposition) /ˌvi:zɑ:ˈvi:/
in relation to.
'Did you hear what the CEO said vis-à-vis trade unions and workers' rights?'

voluntary redundancy (noun) /ˌvɒləntəri rɪˈdʌndənsi/
when an employee is financially incentivised to quit their job as part of a wider reduction in staff.
'I've been offered voluntary redundancy and I'm tempted to accept it.'

W

walk (something) back (phrasal verb) /ˌwɔːk ˈbæk/
to retract something you have said or done.
'The health minister walked back her comments about nurses not being allowed to go on strike.'

wash its face (idiom)
if a product or service washes its face, it makes enough revenue to cover the costs of production.
'Hopefully our new subscription service can wash its face within the next year or two.'

weigh in (phrasal verb) /ˌweɪ ˈɪn/
to enter a discussion and give your opinion or viewpoint.
'Various team members weighed in with their thoughts on who should lead the project.'

weigh (something) up (phrasal verb) /ˌweɪ ˈʌp/
to consider the advantages and disadvantages of a situation in order to make a decision.
'I'm weighing up a couple of job offers I've received.'

wheelhouse (noun) /ˈwiːlˌhaʊs/
an area in which someone has a lot of expertise.
'Digital marketing isn't really in my wheelhouse, so I've brought someone in to help.'

when all is said and done (phrase)
a phrase used to highlight the most important point from a situation.
'When all is said and done, we simply can't pay the same wages as the big Silicon Valley tech firms.'

when push comes to shove (idiom)
at the point at which you are forced to act or make a decision (also 'if push comes to shove').
'Ultimately, when push comes to shove, I would never choose to leave this company, it's become like a second home to me.'

where the rubber meets the road (idiom)
the point at which an idea or theory is put to the test to see if it works in reality.
'We think we've built a great product but it's where the rubber meets the road that will tell us how good it really is.'

whistle-blower (noun) /ˈwɪsəlˌbləʊə/
someone who reports wrongdoing to an authority.
'A whistle-blower has come forward with accusations of widespread bullying and harassment within the firm.'

'wheelhouse'

wiggle room (noun) /ˈwɪgəl ˌruːm/
flexibility or freedom to make small changes to a plan, negotiation, etc. (also 'wriggle room').
'I definitely sense there's a little wiggle room around the asking price.'

'there's a little wiggle room'

wind (something) up (phrasal verb) /ˌwaɪnd ˈʌp/
to end something, e.g. a meeting.
'What time are we planning to wind this meeting up?'

wind (something) up (phrasal verb) /ˌwaɪnd ˈʌp/
to close down a business.
'Sadly, they've had to wind up the old bookshop in town.'

wing (something) (verb) /wɪŋ/
to do something without any preparation, e.g. give a presentation.
'My laptop died while I was giving my presentation, so I had to wing it.'

win (someone) over (phrasal verb) /ˌwɪn ˈəʊvə/
to convince someone that your argument or point of view is the correct one (also 'win (someone) round').
'Abdul didn't want to run another A/B test, but I managed to win him over.'

win-win situation (noun) /wɪnˈwɪn sɪtʃuˌeɪʃən/
a result in which everyone benefits (also 'win-win').
'If they buy our company and keep on all the staff, it'll be a win-win situation for everybody.'

word of mouth (phrase)
if information is passed by word of mouth, one person tells another person, who tells another person, and so on. Recommendations are often spread this way.
'For all the advertising we do, it's still word-of-mouth recommendations that bring us the most business.'

workaround (noun) /ˈwɜːkəˌraʊnd/
a way to overcome a problem, usually temporarily.
'The projector doesn't seem to be working in the boardroom, so we need to figure out a workaround.'

workflow (noun) /ˈwɜːkˌfləʊ/
the sequence of steps that takes a piece of work from beginning to end.
'Ella and I have put together a really clear workflow for the team to follow.'

working group (noun) /ˈwɜːkɪŋ ˌgruːp/
a small group of people brought together to work on a specific issue or common goal.
'Let's set up a working group to manage the office relocation.'

‘work–life balance’

work–life balance (noun) /ˌwɜːk laɪf ˈbæləns/
the division of time between work and recreational activities.
‘My work–life balance has been terrible since starting this new job.’

work (something) out (phrasal verb) /ˌwɜːk ˈaʊt/
to calculate the answer to a mathematical problem.
‘We need to go back through the invites and work out how many people we’ve invited to the conference.’

work (something) out (phrasal verb) /ˌwɜːk ˈaʊt/
to find a solution by thinking or talking about a problem or puzzling situation.
‘If took us some time to work out what was causing the fall in profits.’

work (one’s) socks off (idiom)
used to say someone works very hard. There are less polite alternatives that replace ‘socks’, but I’ll leave those to your imagination.
‘I’ve been working my socks off trying to get this policy update done before I go off on holiday tomorrow.’

workstream (noun) /ˈwɜːkˌstriːm/
a collection of tasks that are to be completed by different groups, in order to achieve a common goal.
‘We’ve set up a communications workstream to deliver a brand-new system.’

wrap (something) up (phrasal verb) /ˌræp ˈʌp/
to bring something to an end.
‘OK team, to wrap things up I thought it would be nice to share one key learning from today.’

Y

year-on-year (adjective) /ˌjɪəɒnˈjɪə/
used to compare numerical results at the same point every year (also 'year-over-year'). You can adapt this format to say 'week-on-week' or 'month-on-month'.
'Our unsubscribe rates have increased year-on-year ever since we started emailing twice a day.'

Z

zero-hours contract (noun) /ˌzɪərəʊ aʊəz ˈkɒntrækt/
a contract that guarantees zero hours of work. It's designed to be flexible for both employer and employee, especially in situations where the amount of work fluctuates.
'I'm on a zero-hours contract at the moment because I'm also studying for a master's degree.'

zoom in on (something) (phrasal verb) /ˌzuːm ˈɪn ɒn/
to take a very close look at something.
'If we zoom in on the numbers for last year, we can clearly see a trend to the upside.'

zoom out (phrasal verb) /ˌzuːm ˈaʊt/
to take a wider, less detailed look at something.
'When you zoom out and look at the overall economic landscape, I'd say we are in a healthy position.'

'zero-hours contract'

BUSINESS ACRONYMS AND INITIALISMS

In a world where time is money, brevity is gold. So, in an effort to communicate more concisely, we employ the help of acronyms and initialisms.

We form acronyms by taking the first letter of every word in a phrase, e.g. ASAP = as soon as possible. When it is used in spoken English, we say it as a word – ASAP /ˈeɪsæp/.

We form initialisms the same way, e.g. IPO = initial public offering. However, when we say them, we pronounce each letter – IPO /ˌaɪ piː ˈəʊ/.

Most of the words in this list are initialisms; I've asterisked (*) the acronyms.

TOM'S TIPS

It's worth noting that not everyone you communicate with in a work context will be familiar with all of these terms. To be honest, using them can be a bit of a minefield. So my advice to you is to use the full phrase the first time it's mentioned, e.g. project manager, and then the acronym or initialism from then on, i.e. PM.

AGM annual general meeting

AL annual leave

AOB any other business

ASAP* as soon as possible

B2B back-to-back

B2B business to business

B2C business to consumer

BYOD bring your own device

CDO	chief data officer
CEO	chief executive officer
CFO	chief financial officer
CIO	chief information officer
CMO	chief marketing officer
COB	close of business
COO	chief operations officer
COP	close of play
CPD	continuing professional development
CRM	customer relationship management
CSR	corporate social responsibility
CTA	call to action
CTO	chief technology officer
CTR	click-through rate
DEI	diversity, equity and inclusion
DM	direct message
DOE	depends on experience
EA	executive assistant
EOB	end of business
EOD	end of day
EOM	end of month
EOP	end of play
EOW	end of week
ERG	employee resource group
ESG	environmental, social and governance
ETA	estimated time of arrival
FAQ	frequently asked question
FYI	for your information
GDPR	general data protection regulation
HQ	headquarters
HR	human resources

HRM	human resource manager
IMO	in my opinion
IP	intellectual property
IPO	initial public offering
IT	information technology
KPI	key performance indicator
LLC	limited liability company
M&A	mergers and acquisitions
MBA	master of business administration
MD	managing director
MNC	multinational corporation
MO	modus operandi
MTD	month-to-date
NDA	non-disclosure agreement
NP	no problem
NSFW	not safe for work

OOO	out of office
P&L	profit and loss
PA	personal assistant
PAYE	pay as you earn
P/E	price to earnings ratio
PM	project manager
PO	purchase order
PPT	PowerPoint presentation
PR	public relations
Q1	quarter one
Q2	quarter two
Q3	quarter three
Q4	quarter four
Q&A	question and answer
QTD	quarter-to-date
R&D	research and development
ROI	return on investment
SEO	search engine optimisation
SMART*	specific, measurable, achievable, relevant, time-bound
SWOT*	strengths, weaknesses, opportunities, threats
SXO	search experience optimisation
T&Cs	terms and conditions
TBA	to be announced
TBC	to be confirmed
TBD	to be determined
TOIL*	time off in lieu
TOS	terms of service
USP	unique selling point
UX	user experience
VA	virtual assistant
VP	vice president
WC	week commencing
WFH	work from home
YTD	year-to-date

MINI LESSONS

Contents

Mini Lesson 1

INTRODUCING WHAT YOU DO

Answering the question 'What do you do?' can be hard enough in your own language, let alone in English. So in this Mini Lesson, we are going to look at a few straightforward structures that will help you to introduce and explain lwhat you do.

Of course, not everyone has a job, so here are some alternative ways to describe what you do.

I'm a student *(someone studying)*

I'm a homemaker *(manages a home/childcare)*

I'm a stay-at-home mum/dad/parent *(manages a home/childcare)*

I'm in between jobs right now *(no current job)*

I'm currently looking for work *(no current job)*

I'm unemployed *(no current job)*

I'm out of work *(no current job)*

If you do have a job, there are a few ways you might answer 'What do you do?'

I'm a + job *'I'm an accountant/a nurse/a freelance journalist/a plumber.'*

Or you can use the word 'work' in various different ways:

I work as a + job

'I work as a teacher in a school.'

'I work as a consultant for Deloitte.'

There are also other prepositions you can use with 'work' to describe your job.

work for + name of company
'I work for Google.'

work at + name of company
'I work at Google.'

work for + type of company
'I work for a tech company.'

work at + type of company
'I work at a tech company.'

work in + industry/field/department
'I work in tech.'

work in + building
'I work in a school.'

YOUR TURN

What do you do?

Mini Lesson 2

EXPLAINING WHAT YOU DO

Once we've told someone what we do, they might follow up with questions like:

'What does that involve?' or *'Doing what exactly?'*

This is a chance to expand on what we've said and give more details about the main tasks and responsibilities of our job:

'I work in data analysis for YouTube. I head up the European division.'

or

'I work in HR at a bank. I'm responsible for recruitment and payroll.'

You might want to use expressions like:

'I spend most of my time + (activity)' or 'My job involves + (activity)'

There are also a number of helpful verbs and verb phrases we can use to explain our job roles and tasks.

head (something) up
to take charge or lead something, e.g. a project, department or business.
'Charmaine heads up our IT team in Spain.'

be responsible for (something)
to be in control of something.
'I'm responsible for all teacher training and professional development at the school.'

deal with (something)
to take action or make decisions to achieve something or solve problems.
'It's my job to deal with all the customer service complaints we receive.'

oversee
to watch or organise something to make sure it is done well.
'She oversees the sales team in Ireland.'

help with (something)
to make it easier for someone/a company to do something.
'I help with any social media work that needs to be done.'

run
to be in control of something.
'I've been running this business for over ten years.'

handle
to take responsibility for something.
'I handle all the repairs and maintenance onboard the yacht.'

take care of (something)
to take responsibility for something.
'I take care of all the team social events throughout the year.'

OK, let me try and describe what I do:

'I'm a YouTuber and I run a business that's wrapped around my channel. I teach English as a second language to people around the world and I spend most of my time designing and creating engaging lessons. I oversee a small team who help me with marketing, social media and new product launches.'

YOUR TURN

Describe your job and what you have to do:

Mini Lesson 3

COMMUNICATING WITH COLLEAGUES (POLITE REQUESTS)

As I mentioned earlier in the book, being polite and professional are fundamental to communicating in the workplace. Brits are known for their indirectness, which can be a source of frustration for those not used to it, but it's our way of trying to be polite. A rule of thumb that I often talk about is 'the longer the sentence, the politer it is'. Look at this sliding scale of requests and notice how they get politer as they get longer.

DIRECT

'Pen!'

'Can I borrow a pen?'

'Can I borrow a pen, please?'
'Could I borrow a pen, please?'

'Would you mind if I borrowed a pen?'

'I'm sorry to bother you, but would you mind if I borrowed a pen?'

INDIRECT

Now, of course, you don't need to use language like this all the time. Simply knowing a few useful structures to 'fluff up' your words can go a long way to sounding more polite. Here are some you can use to make polite requests.

Making polite requests

Would you mind + verb(ing) ...?
'Would you mind opening the window?'

Do you mind + verb(ing) ...?
'Do you mind giving me a hand with this presentation?'

Could you + infinitive ...?
'Could you send me an email confirmation?'

When making a request, it's quite common to put an additional phrase at the beginning to soften the request. It often acknowledges how busy the other person is, e.g. 'When you have a moment …'.

'When you get the chance, would you mind …?'

'When you have a moment, could you …?'

'If you've got a spare minute, would you mind …?'

'If it's not too much trouble, do you mind …?'

If you aren't sure if someone can do something, you can use this structure:

I don't suppose you could + (request)

'I don't suppose you could help with the event this evening?'

Another structure that is sometimes used, especially when requesting favours, is:

You wouldn't …, would you?

'You wouldn't be able to lead the meeting this afternoon, would you?'

You couldn't …, could you?

'You couldn't help out at the fundraiser tonight, could you?'

In written English, a structure you'll see a lot is:

would be grateful if + (request)

'I would be grateful if you could forward this email on to your manager.'

YOUR TURN

Make these direct requests politer by using some of the structures on pages 100 and 101:

Direct – 'Call the client.'

____

____

Direct – 'Help me with this IT problem.'

____

____

Direct – 'Organise a staff social event.'

____

____

Mini Lesson 4

COMMUNICATING WITH COLLEAGUES (ASKING FOR PERMISSION POLITELY)

Following on from our previous lesson, we're now going to look at how to ask for permission politely. It's a skill that will help you communicate with colleagues and successfully navigate office life. The same rule applies as the previous lesson; longer structures tend to help form politer sentences. Let's look at a few.

Asking for permission politely:

Would it be OK if ...?
'Would it be OK if I took Thursday off?'

Would you mind if ...?
'Would you mind if I worked from home today?'

Would it be possible ...?
'Would it be possible to rearrange the meeting for later in the day?'

Could I ...?
'Could I come in to work a little late tomorrow?'

May I ...?
'May I leave early today?'

'Notice how we use the past form of the verb after "Would you mind if ...?", e.g. "Would you mind if we looked at this tomorrow?"'

Teacher Tom

YOUR TURN

Use the prompts to ask for permission politely:

Prompt – 'Take holiday in July.'

Prompt – 'Sit in on a meeting.'

Prompt – 'Switch desks.'

Mini Lesson 5

TALKING ABOUT WORKING HARD

In this lesson, we are going to look at various ways to describe how hard you work and how much work you have to do. I've picked out some useful idioms and phrasal verbs from the A–Z dictionary that you'll love.

Having a lot of work to do

One of my favourite ways to talk about having a lot of work to do is **to have a lot / too much on (one's) plate** (idiom). This means that you have too many tasks or activities to do. It's ideal for when your boss asks you to do a million things before yesterday! We can also use it to describe our personal lives, so if you have lots of work plus you need to look after the kids, clean the house, get a birthday present for your mother-in-law and walk the dog ... this is the perfect phrase. Another idiom we could employ is **up to (one's) neck in (something)** (idiom). This means you have more work than you can handle. For example, you could say:

'I'm up to my neck in admin.'

You could also say:

'I'm up to my eyeballs in paperwork.'

A phrase that is equally descriptive is **to be snowed under** (idiom). Again, it means having too much work to do.

'I'm afraid I can't come out tonight. I'm snowed under with work right now.'

Working late

If your job requires you to work late, I've got some great phrases for you. Our first one is **to pull a late one** (phrase), which is an informal way to say 'work very late'. Writing my dissertation at university, I had to pull many late ones!

'I've still got a mountain of work, so it looks like I'm going to have to pull a late one tonight.'

We can also **burn the candle at both ends** (idiom), which means to work or stay up from early in the morning until late at night while not getting enough rest, so that you become exhausted.

'This week I've been burning the candle at both ends doing the early and late shifts while our manager is away.'

If you work late into the night, you could use **burn the midnight oil** (idiom). This phrase comes from a time when people used to get light from oil lamps.

'This new job has me regularly burning the midnight oil.'

And all this hard work might mean you **burn yourself out** (phrasal verb). This means to make yourself unable to work and possibly unwell because you do too much work. Not what anyone wants!

'A lot of YouTubers I know have burned themselves out trying to create content every day.'

Putting in effort and working as a team

We have some wonderful phrases to talk about putting in more effort and working as a team. One of my favourites is **all hands on deck** (idiom). We use this to say that everyone is needed to work hard on something in order to get it done. It's like a call to arms: 'Come on everyone, we need to do this together.'

The etymology comes from the old naval days when a ship's commander would demand all sailors (hands) go on to the deck of the ship to help steer it in stormy conditions.

'We need all hands on deck if we are going to finish this work on time.'

If you **go the extra mile** (idiom), you make an added effort to achieve something.

'It's great to see the interns go the extra mile to prove they deserve a full-time job.'

You could also **bend over backwards** (idiom) for someone, which means you make an extra special effort to do something for them.

'The team has bent over backwards to make this deal happen.'

Finally, it's important to **give a hundred per cent** (idiom), which means to do something with all your effort.

'Everyone needs to give a hundred per cent in these next few weeks as we lead up to the launch.'

YOUR TURN

Fill in the gap to complete the sentence:

1. 'Candice has been a great addition to the team. She's happy to go the extra __________ to get the job done.'
2. 'Sorry I can't come out tonight, I've got far too much on my __________ at work.'
3. 'You look knackered! Have you been burning the __________ oil?'
4. 'My new team has bent __________ backwards to make me feel welcome.'
5. 'I'm completely snowed __________ at the moment. Can I call you back tomorrow?'

Mini Lesson 6

TALKING ABOUT LEAVING AND LOSING A JOB

We've all left or lost a job at one time or another, right? My friend once lost his job because he hadn't shaved that morning. Harsh! Anyway, here are a set of words that are used to describe both leaving and losing a job. Let's start with the former.

Leaving a job

We've got a couple of classics I'm sure you already know, such as **resign** (verb) and **quit** (verb). They are fairly interchangeable.

'The reason I resigned is because I didn't feel supported by management.'

If someone is in a position of responsibility, they might **step down** (phrasal verb), which means to resign from a job/role/position.

'I've decided to step down as social coordinator and let someone else have a go.'

Two more phrases that are commonly used are to **hand in (one's) resignation** (phrase) and **hand in (one's) notice** (phrase), which both mean to tell your employer you intend to leave your job.

'It feels so good to have handed in my notice at work. I'm free!'

Losing a job

When we talk about losing our jobs, we have quite a few verbs, phrases and euphemisms. Two verbs that sound quite direct and to the point are **sack** (verb) and **fire** (verb). Both mean to terminate someone's employment.

'I'm so glad I've never had to sack someone.'

We then have a few terms that are a little softer, **let (someone) go** (phrase) and **lay (someone) off** (phrasal verb). They share the meaning of stopping someone's employment and don't sound quite as harsh and direct as 'sack' and 'fire'.

'The company has let three people go this week and it looks like there will be more to follow.'

If a company wants to terminate someone's employment and set a time period for that to happen, they **give (someone) their notice** (phrase).

'The company I work for is making loads of redundancies and they gave us all two weeks' notice.'

But perhaps the most euphemistic of all the phrases is to **relieve (someone) of their duties/responsibilities** (phrase). It simply means to stop employing someone, but it is a more formal and delicate way of putting it.

'After a turbulent year, the board has decided to relieve the CEO of her duties.'

Gardening leave

Finally, a concept that sounds rather delightful if you ask me is **gardening leave** (noun). This is a period of time after someone leaves a job, when they are still paid by the employer, but can't work or start a new job.

'They have put the CTO on gardening leave for three months' full pay.'

YOUR TURN

Fill in the gap to complete the sentence:

1. 'Many of the big tech firms are laying ____________ staff this year.'
2. 'The board has decided to ____________ the CEO of their duties.'
3. 'I'm going to hand ____________ my notice next week.'
4. 'Did you hear Malik has decided to step ____________ as CFO?'
5. 'They've put a few of the top execs on gardening ____________.'

Mini Lesson 7

TEN ESSENTIAL PHRASAL VERBS FOR BUSINESS

So much of the communication we have with our direct colleagues is done informally through everyday language, and in particular, phrasal verbs. If you aren't familiar with what a phrasal verb is, it's a verb + particle which, when put together, takes on a meaning that is different from its separate parts. So, for example, 'take over' means to start doing a job or responsibility that someone else did before:

'Anna is taking over as chief marketing officer next month.'

They are a tremendous tool for English learners to communicate naturally and informally. Now, when I'm teaching phrasal verbs I usually get my students to raise their hands in the air and shout, **'I love phrasal verbs'**. Don't worry, I won't ask you to do that, but I do hope you start to love them a little more after this mini lesson.

In the A–Z dictionary, there are lots of fabulous phrasal verbs; here are ten super useful ones I've picked out.

Reach out (to someone)

Our first one is an absolute classic, to **reach out to (someone)**. We use this when we are contacting someone in order to talk to them or perhaps offer them help. You might reach out to a colleague, client or friend to discuss a work matter or someone might reach out to you for some help:

'Someone on LinkedIn reached out to me the other day to see if I'd like to apply for a role at The Times.'

Circle back (to something)

Classic work-related phrasal verb number two is **circle back (to something)**, which means to return to a topic/point/suggestion/idea. It's great in meetings when you are bouncing between topics or ideas:

'Let's circle back to this when we've got more data.'

Pencil (something) in

Speaking of meetings, there's a great phrasal verb to make a plan knowing that the details of it might change: **pencil (something) in**. We use it for meetings, catch-ups and any other plan we might make with someone:

'Let's pencil in a meeting for next week.'

Kick (something) off

Continuing the theme of meetings, we use **kick off** as an informal way to say 'begin'. So you might say:

'I'd like to kick this meeting off by thanking everyone for attending during this busy time.'

Wrap (something) up

To bring a meeting to an end we might say **wrap up**:

'Before we wrap this meeting up, does anyone have any questions?'

Follow (something) up

After a meeting there might be the need to find out more about something that was discussed or how something progressed. In this case, you could use **follow (something) up**:

'Can you follow up with their tech team next week and see if they were able to make the changes?'

Chase (something/someone) up

On a similar note, we might need to **chase (something/someone) up**, which means to find out what is being done about something:

'I still haven't heard from our lawyers. Can you chase them up for me?'

Loop (someone) in

It might also be necessary to keep people informed about something that was said in the meeting, so you would then **loop (someone) in**:

'Is there anyone else you want me to loop in to this email chain?'

Iron (something) out

In business, as in life, we sometimes come across problems along the way. One phrasal verb we can use to describe solving those problems is to **iron (something) out**:

'The lawyers just need to iron out a few details in the contract and then we can sign.'

Slack off

And our last one is for those of us who like to take it easy every now and again. **Slack off** is a wonderful informal way of saying you put less effort into your work:

'You'll notice people in the office tend to slack off a little bit on Friday afternoons.'

YOUR TURN

Fill in the gap to complete the sentence:

1. 'Can we pencil ______________ a meeting for Thursday?'
2. 'I've reached ______________ to a few influencers to see if they'd like to collaborate.'
3. 'Let's circle ______________ to our pay review when the CFO is in on Monday.'
4. 'The deal is ready to sign, we just need to iron ______________ a few small details.'
5. 'Can we start wrapping ______________ this meeting. A few of us have training starting shortly.'

Mini Lesson 8

TEN ESSENTIAL VERBS FOR BUSINESS

As I did with phrasal verbs, I've picked out ten super useful verbs that are essential for English learners to know and master. They help with a range of things, from explaining your role more precisely to communicating with colleagues more easily.

Onboard

Our first essential verb is to **onboard (someone)**. This means to make sure a new employee becomes familiar with the skills and knowledge needed to be an effective member of the organisation. It's the step after recruitment where a new colleague is given the help they need to hit the ground running:

'I'm helping to onboard the new grads all this week, so I might not be around that much.'

Liaise

This next verb is all about working with colleagues to share information or do a task collaboratively: **liaise (with someone)**. It's all about cooperation, something we all need to do from time-to-time in our jobs:

'Could you liaise with the marketing team to get some posters made for our launch party?'

Delegate

Sometimes we need to talk about taking control and getting people to do things for us. In this case, we can use the word **delegate**. Essentially, it's choosing someone to do a duty, job or task:

'Why don't you delegate some of the project management tasks to Jack?'

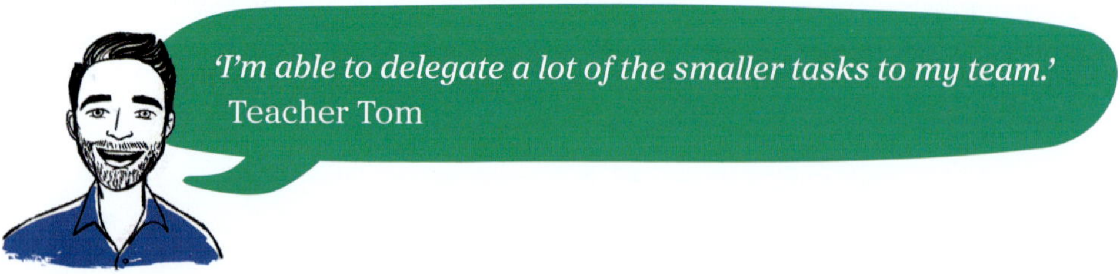

Outsource

In a similar way, we can use **outsource (something)** for when a company gets another company to do the work it needs:

'We've outsourced our customer service centre to a company in the northeast of England.'

Brainstorm

Many jobs are very collaborative and we need to share and generate ideas with each other. A word you may have encountered before is **brainstorm**, which is to generate and suggest ideas to a group:

'We need to sit down and brainstorm fresh ideas for our new ad campaign.'

Float

Another way we suggest plans or ideas is to **float (something)**. This can be quite a tentative plan, and perhaps even a little bit speculative:

'Marta has floated the idea of our team moving to the Canary Wharf office permanently.'

Pitch

One last verb that links to this theme of generating new ideas is to **pitch**. If you **pitch** an idea/suggestion/concept, you present it with the aim of getting approval or financial support. I used to work in TV and we would often be pitching new TV shows to the executives and clients:

'We're pitching our new marketing campaign to the client this afternoon.'

OK

A really simple but effective verb to say that you give someone permission to go ahead with a plan or suggestion is to **OK (something)**:

'Has your manager OK'd your annual leave request?'

Action

Once decisions are made, we need to make them happen. A word that's used to talk about this is to **action (something)**. This means to deal with something or make it happen:

'There are a few points from our meeting that still need to be actioned.'

Flag

When encountering problems or issues, we might want to bring them to the attention of certain people and one word we can use to explain that is to **flag (something)**:

'I just want to flag the possibility that half the team might be on a training day next week.'

YOUR TURN

Fill in the gap to complete the sentence:

1. 'They are thinking of _______________ all the IT support to a company in Sunderland.'
2. 'There are a number of mistakes in my contract that I need to _______________ with HR.'
3. 'As a manager, you are going to need to learn to _______________ work to your team. You can't do it all yourself.'
4. 'I am still waiting for my manager to _______________ my holiday request.'
5. 'My boss _______________ the idea of our team all going down to a four-day week.'

Mini Lesson 9

SUGGESTING IDEAS AND BEING PERSUASIVE

Suggesting ideas

One of the great battles in life is trying to persuade everyone that your ideas are the best. I've tried and failed for years. In the last Mini Lesson, we learned the verb to **float (something)**, which means to suggest a plan or idea. Another favourite of mine is the idiom **run (something) up the flagpole**. It's exactly the same concept of suggesting an idea to see what the reaction is, but it's just a little more descriptive.

'I've got a couple of ideas I'd like to run up the flagpole at the next meeting.'

If you have an idea that you want someone specific to approve or give their opinion on, you could use **run (something) by (someone)**.

'Let's run your plan by HR and see what they say.'

Being persuasive

Those are all great ways to put our ideas forward, but we need to know how to persuade people that our ideas are the best. One lovely little phrasal verb you can use is to **win (someone) over**. It means to persuade someone that your argument or point of view is the correct one.

'Chris said he didn't want to present at the conference, but I'm sure I can win him over.'

Speaking of being persuasive, an idiom that encapsulates this concept of getting someone to agree with you or do what you want them to do is to **twist (someone's) arm**.

'Alright, you've twisted my arm! I'll come to the social for an hour, but then I'm going home.'

One last pair of words that you can use to persuade someone is to **talk (someone) into (something)** and to **talk (someone) out of (something)**. If you talk them into doing something, you persuade them to do it:

'The team has managed to talk me into going to the pub for after work drinks.'

Conversely, if someone talks you out of something, they persuade you not to do it:

'I was close to quitting my job and then my manager had a word and managed to talk me out of it.'

YOUR TURN

Fill in the gap to complete the sentence:

1. 'Hyun-Jae ______________ the idea of us organising a team-building day. What do you think?'
2. 'Before we agree to their proposal, shall we ______________ it by Sarika to get her opinion?'
3. 'Is there any way I can ______________ you out of leaving the company?'
4. 'Initially I didn't think it was a good idea, but they've ______________ me over.'
5. 'Try and ______________ Miki's arm and get her to join us for lunch.'

Mini Lesson 10

TALKING ABOUT TIMES AND DEADLINES

In a world where everything needs to be done ASAP, I thought it was a good opportunity to look at time-specific requests and talk more generally about time and deadlines.

First of all, let's look at ways we might make time-specific requests.

In Mini Lesson 3, we looked at polite requests, so let's use some of those phrases to start us off.

Could you + (request) + time

'Could you / get this to me / by the end of the day?'

'Could you / send me the first draft / before Friday?'

Another way to say this would be:

I would be grateful if + request + time

'I'd be grateful if you could / get this finished / by 4 p.m. this afternoon.'

'I'd be grateful if you could / call head office / at some point today.'

A third request that can be used with a deadline is:

When you have/get the chance + time + request

'When you get the chance / today, / could you go over to the Soho office and pick up a few things?'

'When you have the chance / this week, / would you mind writing a quick bio of yourself for the blog?'

OK, so those are three ways to make time-specific requests. Here are a few informal ways to respond and say you will do the task soon.

I'll + (task) + shortly / in a minute / in a moment / in a second / when I get the chance.

A – 'Could you send me the invoices before the close of play today?'

B – 'Sure thing. I'll send them over shortly.'

A – 'When you get the chance today, could you complete your online training?'

B – 'Absolutely, I'll do it in a minute, after I've sent this email.'

A more formal phrase you might see when setting a deadline is **at your earliest convenience**, which means 'as soon as you have time'. It's most frequently used in written English rather than spoken English.

To finish off, let's look at some idioms related to time and deadlines. When you get things done with very little time to spare before the deadline expires, you can say you've **cut (it/things) fine**:

'We could leave the decision until Friday, but we'd be cutting it fine.'

You could also say **in the nick of time**, which means doing something only just before it needs to happen.

'I managed to get my application to them in the nick of time.'

An idiom to describe doing something in the very last moment that is possible is **the eleventh hour**.

'We didn't think the sale would go through, and then at the eleventh hour new investors came in and the deal was done.'

One final phrase that is very, very informal and quite humorous is **last minute dot com**, which takes its name from the holiday-booking website. It's a fun way to describe someone who does things at the last possible moment. This phrase isn't super common, but it's a fun one to know.

'Lewis is a little last minute dot com for my liking.'

YOUR TURN

Fill in the gap to complete the sentence:

1. 'Thankfully we got the contract signed in the ______________ of time.'
2. 'When you get a ______________, could you call Isla?'
3. 'You haven't finished the PowerPoint! Aren't you ______________ it a little fine?'
4. 'I'd be ______________ if you could send me a copy of the signed contract by tomorrow.'
5. 'I got a call at the eleventh ______________ and changed my mind about leaving here to join Google.'

Mini Lesson 11

PARTICIPATING IN MEETINGS

Whether we like it or not, a large part of our working lives seems to be spent in meetings. Have you ever been in a meeting where the consensus at the end is that you should have more meetings? Ugh! Me too! Anyway, in this lesson, we look at a few useful words and phrases that might help you navigate your way through them successfully. The purpose is to introduce you to common phrases you might hear; if you want to incorporate these phrases into your own spoken English, that's up to you.

Beginning a meeting and welcoming participants

If you are in charge of a meeting, it's important to welcome everyone participating. It's also common to initiate a little small talk, to fill the conversational space before officially starting. This usually involves asking people how they are, talking about the weather and other light topics.

'Hi everyone, thanks for joining us today.'

'Can everybody hear me OK?'

'Let's give everyone a few more minutes to join.'

'Thank you all for being here.'

'How's everyone doing today?'

'Did everyone have a good weekend?'

It may also be necessary to introduce participants in the meeting. You can do this with either:

'Before we get started, let me introduce (name).'

'Before we get started, I'd like to take a moment to introduce (name).'

'Before we get started, let's go around the (table/room/group/call) and introduce ourselves.'

'(Name), would you like to introduce yourself?'

Equally, it's also good to acknowledge any absentees who aren't in the meeting:

'Unfortunately, Valentina can't join us today, she sends her apologies.'

'Just to say, Mike won't be joining us today as he's off-site doing client meetings.'

Getting clarification and understanding

In the age of conference calls and dodgy wi-fi connections, it's only natural that we might struggle to hear everything clearly. Here are a few polite phrases to help you clarify what someone has said:

'Sorry the (line/connection) isn't great, could you repeat that?'

'Sorry (name), could you say that again?'

'Sorry (name), would you mind saying that again?'

'Could you repeat that please (name)?'

'Sorry (name), I didn't catch that last bit. Can you say it again?'

'I'm sorry, could you speak up a bit?' (Asking someone to speak more loudly)

'Would you mind spelling that for me?'

If you feel like you aren't sure what someone is talking about, you can use several phrases to get clarification:

'Would you mind going over that again for me, please?'

'Could you explain that in more detail, please?'

'I'm not sure I fully understand. Would you mind explaining it again for me?'

'What exactly do you mean by ...?'

'Can you just go over that last part again? I'm not sure I completely follow.'

You can also use a technique called paraphrasing to check your understanding. This is when we reword what someone has said, in a shorter way, in order to show that we've understood it correctly.

'If I've understood you correctly, you are saying (paraphrase) ...'

'So, what you are saying is (paraphrase) ...'

'Essentially, are you saying (paraphrase) ...?'

'So, would I be correct in saying (paraphrase) ...?'

Interrupting politely

Unlike some cultures, interrupting isn't seen as the politest thing to do in UK work culture. So when we do need to do it, we must be aware of this and use a softening phrase to introduce our interruption. Here are a few that you could use:

'Could I jump in here ...?'

'Can I just ask ...?'

'Sorry, but just to clarify ...'

'Before we move on, can I just clarify something ...?'

'So what you are saying is ...'

'Sorry to interrupt, but can I just ...?'

'Sorry, I interrupted you. You were saying ...'

Asking for opinions

An important part of a meeting is making sure everyone participates and their opinions are heard. To facilitate this we have some useful phrases to invite people to make contributions:

'What are your thoughts, (name)?'

'I'd love to get your input on this, (name).'

'What's your perspective on this, (name)?'

'(Name), would you like to come in here?'

'Have you got any thoughts, (name)?'

'What do you think about that, (name)?'

'Does anyone have anything else to add?'

Agreeing and disagreeing

One of the most important skills at work is being able to express your opinions in a polite, professional way. We constantly have to agree and disagree with colleagues and clients, so let's look at a few ways to do this.

Agreeing

To show enthusiastic agreement, you could use:

'That's very / so true.'

'Agreed' or *'I agree.'*

'You are absolutely right!'

'I'm with (name) on this ...'

'That makes a lot of sense.'

'For sure.'

'100%.'

'I think that's spot on.'

'Totally!' or *'Absolutely!'*

'I think we are very much (agreed/aligned) on that.'

A slightly more tentative agreement would be:

'I guess (so).'

'I suppose (so).'

'Well, it depends ...'

Disagreeing

We often use a technique of affirming what someone has said and then tactfully introducing other options:

'That's a fair point, but have you considered ...'

'I see/understand your point, but ...'

We then have some slightly more direct responses:

'I'm not so sure (about that).'

'That's not the way I see it.'

'I'm sorry, but ...'

'Not necessarily.'

One final technique we use to disagree is to say 'Do you think so?', with intonation that suggests we are surprised and want to question what they have just said.

'Do you think so? I actually think we are a long way off needing to do that.'

Ending a meeting

Before we end a meeting, there are a few important things we need to do. First, we might need to indicate that there isn't much time left, in which case we can say:

'We're running short on time ...'

'We're a little pressed for time ...'

It's quite common to open up the meeting to allow anyone to add a comment or question at the end:

'Before we wrap up this meeting ...'

'Does anyone have anything else they'd like to discuss?'

'Would anyone like to add anything before we wrap up?'

A few phrases to bring a meeting to an end:

'If nobody has anything else to add ...'

'I think that's everything ...'

'Let's finish there ...'

'Thanks everyone.'

'Thanks all.'

YOUR TURN

Fill in the gap to complete the sentence:

1. 'Sorry, the line isn't great. Could you ______________ that?'
2. 'Can everyone ______________ me OK?'
3. 'Would anyone like to add anything before we______________ up?'
4. 'We're running______________ on time.'
5. 'Sorry Stefanie, I didn't ______________ that last bit. Can you say it again?'

Mini Lesson Answers

MINI LESSON 3

Here are some suggested answers, but there are many more possibilities!

1. 'When you get the chance, would you mind calling the client?'
2. 'If it's not too much trouble, do you mind helping me with this IT problem?'
3. 'I don't suppose you could organise a staff social event?'

MINI LESSON 4

Here are some suggested answers, but there are many more possibilities!

1. 'Would it be OK if I took holiday in July?'
2. 'Would it be possible to sit in on a meeting?'
3. 'Would you mind switching desks?'

MINI LESSON 5

1. mile 2. plate 3. midnight 4. over 5. under

MINI LESSON 6

1. off 2. relieve 3. in 4. down 5. leave

MINI LESSON 7

1. in 2. out 3. back 4. out 5. up

MINI LESSON 8

1. outsourcing 2. flag 3. delegate 4. OK 5. floated

MINI LESSON 9

1. floated 2. run 3. talk 4. won 5. twist

MINI LESSON 10

1. nick 2. chance 3. cutting 4. grateful 5. hour

MINI LESSON 11

1. repeat 2. hear 3. wrap 4. short 5. catch

You're not finished just yet! You can find my Essential Guide to Professional Email Writing with six more Mini Lessons here:

Teacher Tom